FRANK MUIR GOES INTO...

FRANK MUIR AND SIMON BRETT

D0097419

A STAR BOOK
published by
The Paperback Division of
W. H. Allen & Co. Ltd

A Star Book
Published in 1979
by the Paperback Division of W. H. Allen & Co. Ltd
A Howard and Wyndham Company
44 Hill Street, London W1X 8LB

First published in Great Britain by Robson Books Ltd., 1978

Picture research by Juliet Scott

Designed by Harold King

Photos of Frank Muir by Gemma Levine

Printed in Great Britain by Hunt Barnard Web Offset, Aylesbury, Bucks.

ISBN 0 352 30417 0

Permission to use extracts from the following copyright material is gratefully
acknowledged: *Funny Ha Ha and Funny Peculiar* and *Even More Funtastic* by Denys
Parsons (Pan Books); *Most Ruthless Rhymes for Heartless Homes* by Harry Graham
(Edward Arnold); *This England* by Michael Bateman (Statesman and Nation Publishing
Co.); 'The Python' by Hilaire Belloc from his *Cautionary Tales* (Gerald Duckworth);
other Belloc verses and J. B. Morton quotations (A. D. Peters); *It Must Be True* by Denys
Parsons (Macdonald & Co.).

Picture sources: The Witt Library, Courtauld Institute of Art (p.11); Mary Evans Picture
Library (pp. 21, 69, 81, 85, 111, 128); *The Diary of a Nobody* (pp. 14, 15); Victoria &
Albert Museum (pp. 32, 33, 74, 86-87, 134); Radio Times Hulton Picture Library
(pp. 41, 105, 123, 131); *Punch* (pp. 6, 23, 27, 35, 50, 52, 61, 62, 64, 66, 75, 95, 103, 106,
109, 120); Homer Sykes (pp. 57, 137); GEC (p. 31); Weidenfeld & Nicolson (pp. 17, 20,
45, 56, 71, 72, 77); MCC (p. 116); Bamforth Marketing Co. (p. 79); The Mansell
Collection (pp. 43, 88, 97, 140-141); London Editions (pp. 113, 117, 118).

-CONTENTS-

-PREFACE-

Serendipity — that beautiful word coined by Horace Walpole to describe the phenomenon of happy things happening to one when one is intent on doing something else — was the making of a radio show called 'Frank Muir Goes Into...' which is the basis of this book. In fact it is difficult to think of any radio series which enjoyed such serendipulosity — an ugly word which I have just coined.

It all began when BBC Radio 4, seeking to find ways to make use of the mass of recorded material in their archives, asked me to do a Christmas programme for children tracing the development of radio comedy since the War. This went out in 1971 under the title 'Why Are You Laughing?'. It was produced by a couple of likely lads named David Hatch and Simon Brett, who spent hours in listening rooms hearing playbacks of the Golden Oldies of radio, and comedy LPs made by the likes of Woody Allen, Michael Bentine and Stanley Baxter. A group of actors played 'live' sketches and told the sort of jokes which needed to be told as illustrations.

The show did its job. Then came Serendipity One. It became clear that the formula, the 'mix' of the show, was unusual and had more potential than being merely a way of re-broadcasting archive material. So the BBC decided to have a go at a series. It was called 'Frank Muir Goes Into...' because each week we took a theme, e.g., Home, Sport, Jobs, and took a look at the humour which these subjects attracted.

Serendipity Two happened when Alfred Marks joined us. We needed a kind of general-purpose joke-teller and actor and Alfred is a little more than these. He happens to know every old joke (old jokes are vitally important) and can tell them as well as anybody but he is also a fine straight actor, a sensitive reader of poetry and is possessed of an unbelievable range of dialects and accents. As well as his splendid Dr Johnson, with a fine Lichfield accent, and his readings of Mark Twain and Thomas Hood, I cherish the moment when Simon Brett – by now producer – said to Alfred, who was reading a verse of cockney doggerel, 'I'd like it a bit nearer Streatham than Bermondsey.' And got it.

Serendipity Three was having Simon Brett to compile and produce the show. Realising that the lad in charge was one of the New Breed of producers – Simon is an actor and writer (four crime novels and a West End musical so far) as well as a radio and television producer – I came to an arrangement whereby we should share the workload between us. It seemed to me to be a fair arrangement: he did ninety per cent of the work and I did ten per cent (well, he's *younger*).

This book is our attempt to put that same 'mix' onto the printed page, with pictures from the archives in place of sounds. Perhaps – oh, joy! — serendipity will strike again and our book will be read by millions. It's possible, you know. We have already made a start because at least one person – yourself – has got as far as reading the Preface.

-THE HOME-

LUXURY
FLATS
FOR
SALE
OR TO
TAKE
AWAY

Reading

A young couple went to the building society. 'Excuse me,' said the husband. 'I earn £20 a week. How do we stand for a mortgage?'

'You don't,' said the clerk. 'You grovel.'

'Could I speak to the landlord, please?'
'Speaking.'
'It's about the roof . . .'
'Yes?'
'We'd like one.'

An Irish decorator was painting a house and the owner came home to find the man rushing about like a mad thing with his brushes. 'Why are you working so fast?' he asked.

'Well, you see, sor, the paint's running low and I want to finish the job before it's all gone.'

I was clipping the hedge with electric cutters the other day when my neighbour popped his head over to say 'Peep-Bo'. He only got as far as 'Peep'.

Our house is semi-detached. The walls are so thin you can hear the neighbours changing their minds.

A Scotsman was stripping his wallpaper when his friend came round to see him. 'Ah, Andrew,' said the friend, 'are you decorating?'

'No. Moving.'

Everyone has a different ideal home. For some it's anywhere they hang their hat, or where the heart is; others favour a home on the range, an old Kentucky home or a home where the buffalo roam. It doesn't actually make much difference what the ideal is, because very few people find it. Most end up accepting some sort of compromise.

But happily the compromise is quickly forgotten. An Englishman's home *is* his castle and, settled in the sort of semi he swore he'd never go near a year before, the Englishman is lord of all he surveys, from the dolphin door-knocker at the front, all the way over twenty foot of garden to the refuse dump at the end. Pride wells in his heart when he thinks of home. In the words of John Arbuthnot (who was a Scottish Gentleman):

Hame's hame, be it never so hamely.

Home thoughts, either from abroad or from this country, have prompted many people to wax lyrical. People like Oliver Goldsmith:

Such is the patriot's boast, where'er we roam,
His first, best country ever is, at home.

Or like Hannah Moore:

The sober comfort, all the peace that springs
From the large aggregate of little things;
On these small cares of daughter, wife, or friend,
The almost sacred joys of home depend.

Along with the illusion of the ideal home, there's another popular myth – that of 'a home of your own'. In many cases, 'a home of the building society's' is a more accurate description.

But in spite of the prospects of compromises and possible disillusionments, house-hunting remains a popular national pastime. Against all the odds, the Englishman is determined to find

8

his castle and, to that end, he gazes in estate agents' windows and reads their advertisements. It's difficult to know how much to believe of what estate agents advertise. They have been guilty of serious debasement of the English language, diluting superlatives and avoiding pejorative overtones so assiduously that meaning is often totally obscured. No one should venture on the business of house-buying before they understand the language of estate agency. Here is a handy glossary:

ESTATE AGENTESE	ENGLISH
Unique opportunity to purchase...	We are having difficulty in selling
an interesting...	an ugly...
compact...	very small...
cottage-style...	poky...
residence in need of a little enhancement...	house, which is falling down...
situate...	situated...
in exclusive quiet area.	a long way from the shops and public transport.
This unique property...	This house, which is just like all the others in the road...
comprises spacious hall, 2 recep., 2 bdms and mod. kit...	comprises small hall, 2 reception rooms, 2 bedrooms and moderately squalid kitchen...
and many preserved period features.	with no bathroom and an outside loo.

Maybe it's safer to steer clear of estate agents and hope to effect a private purchase by scanning the small ads of a local paper. Here the problems of misleading language are compounded by the fact that some of the goods on offer sound so very unlikely. A few examples:

> **For Sale.**
> Honeymoon cottage;
> sleeps three.

> **For Sale** Here is an opportunity to purchase a charming house at a price which bears no relation to its cost.

> **For Sale** Three-bedroomed terraced house. Fully renovated sitting tenant in basement.

> **For Sale** Well-maintained Edwardian house with guaranteed dry rot throughout.

In desperation the prospective home-buyer may even advertise himself:

> **Wanted** Abingdon. Modern house with three bedrooms and garage space for schoolmaster.

Of course, there are other ways of buying and selling houses. Here's an Irish system, mentioned by Jonathan Swift:

> **I have heard of a man who had a mind to sell his house, and therefore carried a piece of brick in his pocket which he shewed as a pattern to encourage purchasers.**

If you are well off, it is possible to have your own house built and it might be thought that this is the perfect solution to getting an ideal home. Alas, even here there are problems. For a start, your ideas may not coincide exactly with those of your architects. Theirs is a complicated science. Philip Johnson wrote in *The New York Times*:

> **Architecture is the art of how to waste space.**

And you can be sure that, if you start building your own place, your expenses will mount in a way that you never envisaged. Here's Ambrose Bierce's definition of an architect (taken from his *Devil's Dictionary*):

One who drafts a plan of your house and plans a draft of your money.

More succinctly, Dr Johnson expressed his opinion on the matter:

To build is to be robbed.

Given this distrust of the building trades and professions, it is hardly surprising that a lot of ideal-home-seekers, however extensive their means, choose to convert an existing property rather than build a new one. With a few walls knocked down and a bit of imagination, a grotty little two-up-and-two-down with no space can become a fashionable Victorian cottage-style town-house with no space.

But renovation can be an expensive business, too. Here's a warning from the early eighteenth-century playwright, Colley Cibber:

Old houses – mended,
Cost little less than new, before they're ended.

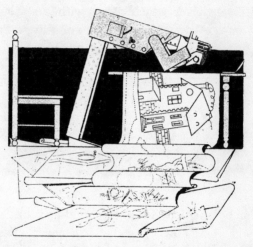

The solution to the problem of creating a dream environment that is becoming increasingly popular is Do-It-Yourself, the theory being that, since the services of skilled workmen cost so much and since your own unskilled services cost so little, who cares about a few bruised thumbs, flooded kitchens and broken marriages? This theory is responsible for all those elliptical cupboards, bubbly wallpapers, diagonal bookshelves and weeping sink units that distinguish the ideal home of the Do-It-Yourself fanatic. Let all such be warned by this cautionary tale from Hilaire Belloc:

> **Lord Finchley tried to mend the Electric Light**
> **Himself. It struck him dead: And serve him right!**
> **It is the business of the wealthy man**
> **To give employment to the artisan.**

Not that the artisan is completely infallible. First you have to get him to agree to come to your home. That in itself is no easy task and is best achieved by dropping to your knees and proffering five-pound notes. And even when he comes, things may not go smoothly. After a few rounds of can't-be-dones, never-seen-one-like-this-befores and can't-get-the-parts-because-of-a-disputes, there's a temptation to go running into rented accommodation.

But when you rent, you don't get everything. You don't get that feeling of total privacy which comes with a place of your own (depending on the sort of neighbours you have). Privacy is all-important. In the words of Benjamin Franklin:

> **Love your neighbour, yet don't pull down your**
> **hedge.**

A man can do as he likes unchallenged in his own home. It's the one place where you should be able to behave quite naturally and that is true even of the highest in the land. Here's a report from the magazine *She*:

> **Blenheim Palace is a famous showplace, but the**
> **Duke can often relax enough to throw raspberries to**
> **the ceiling in the fabulous dining hall and catch**
> **them in his mouth. 'I know by the applause when**
> **he's at it,' says the Duchess.**

Another freedom which comes with a home of one's own is the choice of what it should look like. One can decorate it exactly as one chooses. Indeed the first thing most people do when they move house is to paint or wallpaper away all traces of the previous occupants. On the subject of paint, here's an extract from the diary

13

of Charles Pooter, written at the end of the last century and called by its authors, George and Weedon Grossmith, *The Diary of a Nobody:*

In consequence of Brickwell telling me his wife was working wonders with the new Pinkford's enamel paint, I determined to try it. I bought two tins of red on my way home. I hastened through tea, went into the garden and painted some flower-pots. I called out Carrie, who said: 'You've always got some new-fangled craze'; but she was obliged to admit that the flower-pots looked remarkably well. Went upstairs into the servant's bedroom and painted her washstand, towel-horse, and chest of drawers. To my mind it was an extraordinary improvement, but as an example of the ignorance of the lower classes in the matter of taste, our servant, Sarah, on seeing them, evinced no sign of pleasure, but merely said 'she thought they looked very well as they was before.'

Got some more red enamel paint (red, to my mind, being the best colour), and painted the coal-scuttle, and the backs of our Shakespeare, the binding of which had almost worn out.

Painted the bath red, and was delighted with the result. Sorry to say Carrie was not, in fact we had a few words about it. She said I ought to have consulted her, and she had never heard of such a thing as a bath being painted red. I replied: 'It's merely a matter of taste.'

Fortunately, further argument on the subject was stopped by a voice saying, 'May I come in?' It was only Cummings, who said, 'Your maid opened the door, and asked me to excuse her showing me in, as she was wringing out some socks.' I was delighted to see him, and suggested we should have a game of whist with a dummy, and by way of merriment said: '*You* can be the dummy.' Cummings (I thought rather ill-naturedly) replied: 'Funny as usual.' He said he couldn't stop, he only called to leave me the *Bicycle News*, as he had done with it.

Another ring at the bell; it was Gowing, who said he 'must apologise for coming so often, and that one of these days *we* must come round to *him*.' I said: 'A very extraordinary thing has struck me.' 'Something funny, as usual,' said Cummings. 'Yes,' I replied; 'I think even *you* will say so this time. It's concerning you both; for doesn't it seem odd that Gowing's always *coming* and Cummings' always *going?*' Carrie, who had evidently quite forgotten about the bath, went into fits of laughter, and as for myself, I fairly doubled up in my chair, till it cracked beneath me. I think this was one of the best jokes I have ever made.

The Diary of a Nobody captures the essence of suburbia – rows of almost identical houses set very close together and yet each one a family island from which local events can be surreptitiously observed.

Watching the neighbours is probably the most popular suburban pastime and it can take on obsessive proportions, particularly in the matter of possessions. Keeping up with the Joneses is a depressingly strong motive in many home lives and the domestic calm can be all too easily shattered by the arrival next door of a new car or a colour television. This acquisitive paranoia reflects extreme feelings of inferiority. Here's a letter first published in the magazine *Reynolds News:*

> **Is any other reader afraid of the dustmen? When they call I always hide, just in case they say anything about the type of rubbish I put in the bin.**

The same paper also supplies much useful information to home-owners, such as this tip on the protection of the family house:

> **As soon as you know an H-bomb is on the way, run out and paint your windows with a mixture of whitewash and curdled milk to deflect dangerous rays. Soak your curtains and upholstery with a solution of borax and starch to prevent fire.**

What a useful little gobbet of information. But the house-owner should be prepared for every eventuality. A threat to your house is a threat to you. A home is not just bricks and mortar; it is an expression of your personality. Everything you put in it tells something about you. There are amateur psychologists who can read volumes from possessions. Plaster ducks flying towards the picture rail or television lamps in which great globules of coloured oils glurp up and down can tell more than two hours on the consulting couch. There are clues to personality in Monarch of the Glen table mats and wrought-iron drinks trolleys. Crinoline lady toilet-roll covers, riding crop bottle-openers and Mona Lisa ashtrays all tell something about the person who bought them and wishes to live in a home surrounded by such adornments.

18

'We converted it entirely ourselves, it used to be an eighteenth century windmill.'

What was the Hannah Moore line? 'The large aggregate of little things.' And it's physical little things that make a home. Things that we are constantly battered about by advertisements in colour supplements – little things that will complete our home and make up for any deficiencies in our own personalities. Here's a description of something nobody should be without, from the *Financial Times:*

> **Make the finishing touch the Besca toilet seat, of Polyester foam bonded on to chipboard. Covered in vinyl with an 'antique leather' surface, it is scrubbable in black, white, blue, green, turquoise or pink at 72s 6d. Stuart or Black Watch tartans, bronze, and floral patterns are 77s 6d. So is a Back-Britain model with a white seat and a Union Jack lid.**

What more can anyone ask? Who can doubt that the owner of such a symbol is a person of taste and refinement? Remember, your home is the ultimate expression of YOU and you are judged by your surroundings. Whatever they're like. In the words of Noël Coward:

Be it never so humbug, there's no place like home.

NOTICE TO QUIT.

GEORGE ROLFE.
Broker, &c.,
13a, Pentonville Rd., N

3/6

I hereby Give you Notice to Quit, and yield up to me on or before _Monday_ the _8th_ day of _____ 19_01_, the Quiet and Peaceable Possession of the _Front Kitchen_ situate at No. _____ _Blackfriars_ in the Parish of _Southwark_ in the County of _Surrey_

In failure of your compliance herewith, legal measures will be adopted to compel the same by application at the DISTRICT _Police_ COURT.

Dated this _1st_ day of _____ in the year of our LORD One Thousand Nine Hundred.

Yours, &c., _(Agent)_

(Landlord)

To Mr. _____

The Tenant in Possession _of above_

Witness _____

From LANDLORD to TENANT.

E. REEVES, Printer, 13, Caledonian Road, N.

-MARRIAGE-

A young bride married a handsome older man and was distressed to find out that he had been married three times before. 'But what happened to your other three wives?' she asked.

'Well,' said her husband, 'the first one died from eating poisoned mushrooms.'

'How terrible. And what about the second one?'

'Ah, she died from eating poisoned mushrooms.'

'And the third one?'

'She died of a fractured skull.'

'Oh, that's ghastly,' said the wife.

'Well, it was her own fault. She wouldn't eat the bloody mushrooms.'

VICAR: And how are you and your new wife getting on, George?

GEORGE: Not too good, I'm afraid, vicar. We've separated.

VICAR: But you can't do that. You took her for better or worse.

GEORGE: Yes, vicar, but she was worse than I took her for.

At a rather posh wedding all the presents were displayed and in a prominent position was a cheque for £10,000, a present from the bride's father. As the guests filed past the display, the bridegroom was annoyed to notice one man roaring with laughter at the cheque. 'Who's that?' he asked.

'Oh,' his bride replied, 'it's only Daddy's bank manager.'

'Have you heard, old Henry got married last week.'

'Good. I never liked the fellow.'

A newly-wedded wife was paying her first visit to the butcher. 'What can I do for you, madam?' he asked.

'A pound of steak, please.'

'Yes. There you are. Anything else?'

'Yes. Could I have some gravy too, please?'

'Don't just stand there, help me find the oven. Your supper's in it'

'Young Gladys got married at last.'

'Oh. Who to?'

'A second lieutenant.'

'How's that?'

'The first one got away.'

A man had a wife who was a terrible cook — she just served frozen food day after day. Eventually the husband went to the doctor and explained his problem.

'And what's the trouble?' asked the doctor. 'Ulcers?'
'No, frostbite.'

'Are you married?'
'No, I've always been round-shouldered.'

Marriage is one of the most abused institutions in the world. It seems that nobody has a good word to say for it. Perhaps people who are happily married don't think about it, so comment on the subject is left to the disillusioned and the cynical. Let's look at some of their depressing views. George Jean Nathan:

Marriage is based on the theory that when a man discovers a particular brand of beer exactly to his taste, he should at once throw up his job and go to work in the brewery.

Robert Louis Stevenson:

Marriage [is] a sort of friendship recognized by the police.

George Farquhar:

I don't think matrimony consistent with the liberty of the subject.

Ian Hay:

Marriage is a ghastly public confession of a strictly private intention.

Herbert Spencer:

Marriage: a ceremony in which rings are put on the finger of a lady and through the nose of the gentleman.

And a beautiful image from J. B. Priestley:

Marriage is like paying an endless visit in your worst clothes.

Painted by W. Williams

Aquatinted by F. Jukes

COURTSHIP.

MATRIMONY

27

Considering the shower of vitriolic abuse that has been hurled at it since records began, it is amazing that marriage still survives at all. Perhaps the truth is expressed by Harry Emerson Fosdick:

> **It is not marriage that fails; it is people that fail. All that marriage does is to show people up.**

But, in spite of everything, statistics show that marriage still thrives. Mind you, statistics can show anything. Here's an extract from the Albany *Knickerbocker News:*

> **Before the war 35 per cent of working women were single. Now it's the other way round – 65 per cent are married. A big change in women's lives.**

The motives for marriage vary. Love is still rated quite highly, though that suffers almost as much abuse as wedlock itself. Then there's the profit motive. Marriage is a legal contract with important financial clauses and can be a lifelong meal ticket for a man or a woman. Some opinions maintain the materialistic motive is the best basis. Lord Chesterfield on the subject:

> **There are but two objects in marriage, love or money. If you marry for love, you will certainly have some very happy days, and probably many very uneasy ones; if for money, you will have no happy days and probably *no* uneasy ones.**

As well as abusing the institution, many wits have pointed up the disillusioning difference between the before and after, between courtship and marriage. Lord Byron:

> **Though women are angels, yet wedlock's the devil.**

William Congreve:

> **Courtship [is] to marriage, as a very witty prologue to a very dull play.**

28

'You never tell me you hate me anymore.'

Ken Pyne

The freedom of an affair is always praised above the regularity of marriage. One of the conditions of the courtly love so keenly sought in medieval times was that it was an extra-marital love. But romance has its drawbacks too, as Oscar Wilde observed:

> **Twenty years of romance make a woman look like a ruin; but twenty years of marriage make her something like a public building.**

The reasons that push people over the brink into matrimony vary considerably. A report from the old *Daily Graphic*:

> **A marriage at Merthyr. Magistrate to a woman who sought a maintenance order: 'Do you love your husband?'**

'No. I married him out of spite. I have been let down twice. I determined the next man who asked me had had it.'

Or a letter from the old *Daily Herald*:

I fell in love with my husband simply because he was so different from every other boy I had ever met. He did not like love-making and neither do I. He has never actually told me he loves me...He never actually proposed, but we saw a three-piece suite we liked and that clinched the idea.

But there are other reasons for getting married. For some people the centre of marriage is bed. A little verse by Osbert Mint:

A double bed is one in which
Every time you move a—
Bout, you feel an angry twitch
And lose a bit more duvet.

Whatever their motives, the majority of people do get married. And I'm sure the majority of people couldn't define their motives anyway. Marriage just happens. A casual question can start the whole Centurion tank of relations and arrangements rolling with dreadful momentum – and heaven help the person who tries to halt its progress.

Sometimes the parents are to blame. Even in modern times parents like to engineer their children's matches and there are still many who feel it's part of their parental duty to marry off their offspring – and their daughters in particular. In the eighteenth century it was much worse, as this anonymous rhyme shows:

These panting damsels, dancing for their lives,
Are only maidens waltzing into wives.
Those smiling matrons are appraisers sly,

> **Who regulate the dance, the squeeze, the sigh,**
> **And, each base cheapening buyer having chid,**
> **Knock down their daughters to the highest bid.**

There are still parts of the world where wives can be bought, but in England the commercial nature of the contract is not advertised. Forthcoming marriages are announced on the social page, not in the stock market report. Mind you, in these announcements and in their accounts of weddings, newspapers do not always avoid the ridiculous. Let's have some examples:

> **The bride's father is proprietor of an old-fashioned meat business...The bride wore a gown of white satin fashioned with short leg of mutton sleeves...**

> **The bridesmaids' dresses were pretty combinations of blue and pink.**

> **Hugh and Ruth went to grammar school together and their marriage will stop a romance begun between them there.**

> **The marriage of Miss Anna Bloch and Mr Willis Dashwood, which was announced in this paper a few weeks ago, was a mistake and we wish to correct it.**

Once the wedding is over, the protagonists – or in some cases protagonist and antagonist – immediately change status. They cease to be an engaged couple and suddenly become honeymooners or newly-weds, both popular butts for jokers. Here are a few old favourites on the perennial subject:

> **A couple arrive at the hotel for the first night of their honeymoon and they go up to the bedroom. The husband undresses and gets into bed.**

But the wife doesn't join him. Instead, she sits looking out of the open window at the sky. After a while the husband says, 'Won't you come to bed, darling?'

'Oh no,' says the wife.

'Why not?'

'Well, my mother said this would be the best night of my life and I don't want to miss a minute of it.'

'Darling, darling,' said the newly-wedded husband to his wife, 'I didn't say you were a bad cook. I just said our dustbin had got ulcers.'

A young couple were given every sort of labour-saving device for their wedding. The husband came home from work the first day after the honeymoon and found his new wife crying her eyes out in front of the brand-new washing machine. 'Why, darling, whatever's the matter?' he asked.

'I've tried everything,' she sobbed, 'and I still can't get a picture on this television.'

'I'm sorry about the eggs, darling,' said the young
wife to her husband. 'They were frying beautifully,
but then the shells cracked and they spread all over
the pan.'

'Darling, darling,' said the wife, 'I made this cake
all by myself.'
　'Oh,' said the husband, 'and who helped you lift it
out of the oven?'

And so on and so on. Food is very significant in marriage. The way
to a man's heart is supposed to be through his stomach and the
continuous cycle of meals can be a great strain. Here's an
anonymous rhyme:

> The glances over cocktails
> That seemed to be so sweet,
> Don't seem quite so amorous
> Over the Shredded Wheat.

But in spite of all this anti-marriage propaganda in humour, the
institution itself stands up very well. And some couples stay
sentimental and soppy about each other all their lives, continually
giving tokens of their affection. Here's a letter from *Today:*

My husband is a shy man and whenever he brings
flowers home to me he always conceals them under
his bowler hat. As a result they have to be little
flowers like violets or anemones and tend to smell of
brilliantine. Surely there must be some other way
in which self-conscious men cope with this
problem?

The most important quality in any marriage is tolerance. Not
total calm, but a workable antagonism. Arguments are necessary.
A. P. Herbert:

The idea of two people living together for 25 years without an argument suggests a lack of spirit only to be admired in sheep.

Sometimes marriage requires one partner to give way. As Vicki Baum observes cynically:

Marriage always demands the greatest understanding of the art of insincerity possible between two human beings.

But tolerance need not be insincerity. Sometimes it's just a case of accepting one's partner's little idiosyncrasies. A letter from *Good Shopping*:

When my husband reads in bed on warm nights he puts a colander over his head. He says it keeps off the flies, shades his eyes from the light and lets in the air at the same time.

'She'd like to see some rings.'

Accept the little things like that and you're on the way to success in marriage; ready for the give and take that is part of the institution.

And if you are still in any doubt on the subject, here's a famous word of wisdom from the pages of *Punch:*

Mr Punch's advice to young men about to be married: Don't.

-THE FAMILY-

"Just by way of a Change"

Grandfather bought a brand-new hearing aid. 'Do you know,' he said, 'it's so small nobody notices it.'

'That's great,' I said. 'How much did it cost?'

'Half past four,' he replied.

A little girl used always to go out with her father for a drive on Sundays, but one day her father had a cold and so her mother had to take her out. When they returned, the father asked the child if she had had a good time.

'Oh yes,' said the little girl, 'and we weren't overtaken by a single bastard.'

A father was talking to his son. 'Now listen, my boy, from now on you do your own home-work. I'm not going to do any more for you — it's not right.'

'I know,' said the boy, 'but have a shot at it just the same.'

'*Did you plan it, or goof it?*'

'Tell me, young man,' said the father to his prospective son-in-law, 'if my daughter marries you, and I give her a substantial dowry, what have you to offer her in return?'

'I'll give you a receipt.'

I gave my mother-in-law a waterproof, shockproof, antimagnetic, unbreakable watch. She went and lost it.

Did you hear the one about the cannibal who got married and, at the reception, toasted his mother-in-law?

'Oh, Nigel, I hear you buried you mother-in-law last week.'

'Had to . . . she was dead.'

Abe met Izzy again after many years. 'Tell me, Izzy,' he said, 'how much family do you have now?'

'Three boys,' said Abe, 'three boys. One is a professor, the middle one is a surgeon, and the young one is a judge. What about you?'

'Well, Abe, I also have three sons. The eldest is a heavyweight boxer, the second an all-in wrestler, and the third a judo champion. Why don't you bring your boys over? I'll see they get a good hiding.'

A Scot died and left his cousin all the money his cousin owed him.

Most humour about the family is pretty cruel. This doesn't mean that family love does not exist – only that there's nothing very funny about it. As usual the devil has the best jokes and insults are more memorable than praise. Here's a very bitter view of family life from August Strindberg:

The Family – Home of all social evils, a charitable institution for indolent women, a prison workshop for the slaving breadwinner, and a hell for children.

Francis Bacon also issued a warning on the subject:

He that hath wife and children hath given hostages to fortune; for they are impediments to great enterprises, either of virtue or mischief.

And the pride of an ancestral family is not very highly thought of, either. Anthony Hope:

Good families are generally worse than any others.

The family, as an institution, is receiving quite a battering these days. It used to be regarded as one of the great symbols of order. When the natural affections between close relatives ceased to exist, the fabric of society was threatened. But now the family has to resist the daily onslaughts of sociological theories, the erosion of a more mobile population and a spirit of indifference that amounts almost to callousness. Here's an advertisement from a Tipperary newspaper:

FOR SALE
Nine 7-week-old chickens; would sell mother too, if needed.

And yet most families start in hope, before the cynicism creeps in. The idea of starting a family is still highly regarded and few really anticipate the problems that children can bring. Here's a rare example of foresight from an Indian newspaper:

> **In our last week's issue we announced the birth of a son to Mr and Mrs Gilbert Parkinson. We regret any annoyance that this may have caused.**

The arrival of a baby, particularly the first baby, is a major upheaval in any family. The parents have to adjust to the idea that they can no longer do exactly what they want when they want. And they also have to adjust to the idea of considerably less sleep than they used to have. Here, for all hollow-eyed parents, is a little poem by Thomas Hood, entitled 'A Serenade':

> 'Lullaby, oh lullaby!'
> Thus I heard a father cry,
> 'Lullaby, oh, lullaby!
> The brat will never shut an eye;
> Hither come, some power divine!
> Close his lids, or open mine!'
>
> 'Lullaby, oh, lullaby!
> What the devil makes him cry?
> Lullaby, oh, lullaby!
> Still he stares – I wonder why,
> Why are not the sons of earth
> Blind, like puppies, from the birth?'
>
> 'Lullaby, oh, lullaby!'
> Thus I heard the father cry;
> 'Lullaby, oh, lullaby!
> Mary, you must come and try! –
> Hush, oh, hush, for mercy's sake –
> The more I sing, the more you wake!'
>
> 'Lullaby, oh, lullaby!
> Fie, you little creature, fie!
> Lullaby, oh, lullaby!
> Is no poppy-syrup nigh?
> Give him some, or give him all,
> I am nodding to his fall!'

'Lullaby, oh, lullaby!
Two such nights, and I shall die!
  Lullaby, oh, lullaby!
He'll be bruised, and so shall I, –
How can I from bedposts keep,
When I'm walking in my sleep?'

  'Lullaby, oh, lullaby!
Sleep his very looks deny –
  Lullaby, oh, lullaby;
Nature soon will stupefy –
My nerves relax, – my eyes grow dim –
Who's that fallen – me or him?'

Even if the parents can put up with lack of sleep, dirty nappies, rusk-smeared shoulders and so on, they may find the rest of the world less than besotted with their offspring. Many people just don't like children. Here's Dr Johnson on the subject:

> **One cannot love lumps of flesh, and little infants are nothing more.**

Lord Byron:

> **They always smell of bread and butter.**

John Keats:

> **The servants have come for the little Browns this morning – they have been a toothache to me, which I shall enjoy the riddance of – their little voices are like wasps' stings.**

And Edward Lear:

> **I was much distressed by next-door people who had twin babies and played the violin: but one of the twins died, and the other has eaten the fiddle – so all is peace.**

It's just as well that none of the authors quoted had much to do with the upbringing of children. It is a commonplace of modern psychology that childhood influences are very powerful. In some cases the habits of the child carry through into adult life. It can be very difficult to put away childish things. Here's a letter published in the Brighton and Hove *Herald:*

> **What nonsense to suggest, as your women's page did last week, that the use of a dummy is either unhygienic or a bad habit which could become hard for a baby to break. I have derived great comfort from my dummy for over 40 years, and find it gives**

much greater oral satisfaction than the unhealthy cigarette. It is also much cheaper.

Among child-haters opinion is divided whether it is worse to be afflicted by boys or girls. Here's an old German proverb:

A house full of daughters is like a cellar full of sour beer.

Or an alternative view from Lord Rosebery:

All my life I have loved a womanly woman and admired a manly man, but I never could stand a boily boy.

But beware of daughters all the same. Remember the cautionary tale of Lizzie Borden:

> **Lizzie Borden took an axe**
> **And gave her mother forty whacks;**
> **When she saw what she had done**
> **She gave her father forty-one.**

Which bears out the truth of what Tacitus wrote:

The bitterest hatred is that of near relations.

Yes, it's not just the parent-child relationship that offers grounds for resentment. There are all those brothers and sisters and uncles and aunts and cousins to be reckoned with. H. L. Mencken:

Every man sees in his relatives…a series of grotesque caricatures of himself.

Oscar Wilde:

[Relations are] a tedious pack of people who haven't got the remotest knowledge of how to live nor the smallest instinct about when to die.

Let's look at a few relations. Aunts. Here's a Freudian misprint from *The People's Friend:*

Aunts in the house are a serious nuisance and are not easily expelled once they have established a kingdom. Perhaps a chemist in your town could help you.

It's cleaner than Lizzie Borden's method. Here's another ruthless thought on aunts from Harry Graham:

> **Auntie did you feel no pain**
> **Falling from that willow tree?**
> **Could you do it, please, again?**
> **'Cos my friend here didn't see.**

Harry Graham's *Most Ruthless Rhymes for Heartless Homes* are very destructive to family solidarity. Grandmothers:

> **When Grandmamma fell off the boat,**
> **And couldn't swim (and wouldn't float),**
> **Matilda just stood by and smiled.**
> **I almost could have slapped the child.**

And, for Grandmother's birthday, here's a special message from Hilaire Belloc:

> **Dear Grandmamma, with what we give,**
> **We humbly pray that you may live**
> **For many, many happy years:**
> **Although you bore us all to tears.**

But the member of the family who suffers most from the attacks of vicious humour is the mother-in-law, who, along with Englishmen, Irishmen, Scotsmen, milkmen, policemen and commercial travellers, is part of our joke mythology. The distrust of mothers-in-law goes back as far as marriage does. Here's a part of Juvenal's *Sixth Satire:*

> **Be sure, no quiet can arrive**
> **To you, while her Mamma's alive.**

Samuel Butler:

> **One of the strongest proofs of Christ's personal influence over his followers is to be found in the fact of Peter's remaining on friendly terms with him notwithstanding his having healed his mother-in-law.**

While we're on mothers-in-law, perhaps we should have a little parade of mother-in-law jokes for ready reference:

> **'I just bought my mother-in-law a Jaguar.'**
> **'Cor – I thought you didn't like her.'**
> **'I know what I'm doing – it's bitten her twice already.'**

47

A young wife came home one day and found her mother standing in a bucket of water with her finger stuck in the light socket. The young husband was standing by the switch.

'Hello, darling,' said the mother, 'George has had this marvellous idea for curing my rheumatism.'

You know, I don't know what I'd do without my mother-in-law – but it's nice dreaming about it.

I mean, she's not ugly – it's just that when she makes up, the lipstick crawls back down the tube.

She's found a new cheap way of making yoghourt and sour cream – she just buys a bottle of milk and stares at it for a couple of minutes.

'Do you know, my mother-in-law has vanished, just disappeared from home. Just like that.'
'Have you given her description to the police?'
'No, they'd never believe me.'

And so on and so on. I'm sure mothers-in-law have just as good a stock of son-in-law jokes, but the form has never caught on. Still, the older generation have no illusions about their younger relations. Here's an old Northamptonshire rhyme about children:

As tall as your knee they are pretty to see;
As tall as your head they wish you were dead.

Family stresses exist at every level, though they can usually be solved by methods less extreme than Lizzie Borden's. As I said at the beginning of the chapter, there's not a lot of humour in the majority of families, whose members contrive to live harmoniously together. The best lines come from the cynical and dissatisfied. I'll close with one from Samuel Butler:

There are orphanages for children who have lost their parents — oh! why, why, why are there no harbours of refuge for grown men who have not yet lost them?

-CLASS-

'Good Heavens, Lavinia! It says here the East Wing was
burned down last night.'

There was a private soldier who went on sick parade.

'What's the trouble then?' asked the MO.

'Sir, I've got a pain in my abdomen, sir.'

'Now listen, soldier,' said the MO. 'Officers have abdomens, NCOs have stomachs. What you've got is a pain in your belly.'

A titled gentleman decided to economize, so when he left his club, he didn't hail a taxi as usual, he caught a bus instead. And when he got inside, he said to the conductor, '17 Courtchester Square, please. And it's quicker if you go through the park.'

A wealthy earl went salmon fishing in Ireland and after a fortnight without a bite he eventually hooked one small salmon. As Paddy, his ghillie, landed it, the earl said, 'Do you know, that salmon cost me two hundred pounds?'

'Ah,' said Paddy, 'aren't you the lucky man that you didn't catch two.'

A filthy old tramp knocked at the door of a stately home and when the lady of the house opened it, said: 'Please could I have a piece of fruit cake?'

'What do you mean — fruit cake?' said the lady. 'Surely a bit of bread would be better for you?'

'Ah, maybe,' said the tramp, 'but, you see, today's my birthday.'

A majestic Rolls-Royce was reversing into a meter space in London, when a grubby little Mini nipped into the space from behind. The Mini's owner, a brash young man, got out and strolled past the Rolls-Royce saying, 'You have to be young and fast to do that.' The enormous car's owner did not look at the young man; he just continued reversing and squashed the Mini into a tangled heap against the curb. Then he got out and handed the astonished young man a card with his insurance details, saying, 'You have to be old and very rich to do that.'

Middle-class children take riding lessons and dancing lessons; lower-class children take anything that isn't nailed down.

'Mary,' said the lady of the house to her kitchen-maid, 'where's that chicken I told you to heat up?'
  'Well, mam,' Mary replied, 'you told me to heat it up and I've heaten it up.'

The British class system is still very much with us. Although its form changes continually and although some people maintain that there is progress towards a classless society, the barriers and divisions of class remain popular sources of comedy.

And for many class is part of nature. It is part of the order of things – all must observe their degrees. In the words of Ulysses in Shakespeare's *Troilus and Cressida:*

> **Take but degree away, untune that string,**
> **And, hark, what discord follows!**

The discords still sound, the discords of social climbing and impoverished gentility. But now the barriers of class are continually eroded by the power of money. Breeding can, in time, be bought and this makes the definition of classses increasingly difficult. What makes someone a gentleman? Perhaps it's a sort of natural dignity, something from within. Here's the view of Edmund Burke:

> **Somebody has said, that a king may make a nobleman, but cannot make a gentleman.**

Robert Surtees:

> **The only infallible rule we know is, that the man who is always talking about being a gentleman never is one.**

There's a very subtle difference between actually being a gentleman and not being one. Mr Salteena in Daisy Ashford's book *The Young Visiters* shows commendable self-knowledge on the subject:

'I do hope I shall enjoy myself with you...I am partial to the ladies if they are nice, I suppose it is my nature. I am not quite a gentleman but you would hardly notice it.'

There are certain standards by which one can begin to define one's social position – education, accent, use of language and so on. Here's a letter from the old *Sunday Graphic:*

Have I joined the middle classes? I find myself calling my doctor and my solicitor by their Christian names – and that I'm told is a criterion of middle-class establishment.

There are other criteria by which social levels can be assessed. Language can be very revealing. For instance, there's the oft-quoted fact of semantics that in the English language all the words for animals which provide meat have Anglo-Saxon roots, while all the words for meat as it is served up at table come from the French. Thus one sees bulls and calves and sheep in the fields, but one eats beef and veal and mutton (from '*boeuf*', '*veau*' and '*mouton*'). The explanation of this is purely social. After the Norman conquest, the victorious invaders of England dined off the fat of the land, while the natives were relegated to herdsmen and had to look after the animals.

Even now, how one talks about food is an important pointer to one's social status. Heres a little verse by Tom St Brien, entitled 'Evening Meal':

> **My father's middle-class,**
> **While my mother's rather upper,**
> **So she always speaks of dinner**
> **When my father wants his supper;**
> **And when *his* father stays, they never can agree,**
> **'Cause lower-class old Grandpa's always shouting for**
> **his tea.**
> **So while they fight and quarrel, and while each one**
> **argues harder,**
> **All us kids just sneak away and go and raid the**
> **larder.**

Issues of class have long been subjects for discussion. There's the famo   question posed by John Ball in his Blackheath sermon to Wat Tyler's rebels in 1381:

> **When Adam delved and Eve span,**
> **Who was then the gentleman?**

Certainly not Eve. Though one must beware of assuming that all men are equal when stripped of their clothes and symbols of

THE BOND ST. BEAU,

WRITTEN BY
F. W. GREEN ESQ^R

COMPOSED BY
ALFRED LEE.

position. Here's an extract from *Naturist* magazine about a nudist club:

> **Membership is strictly limited as to numbers, so there is no fear that it will ever by overcrowded, or that uncongenial spirits or persons of a low class will ever bring a jarring note into the Club. The Abbey Club meets the needs of those who hitherto have been deterred from joining a naturist club by the fear that they may find as fellow-members some humble employee, the butler, baker, broker or the insurance man. Not that there is anything snobbish about the club.**

It's wonderful how broad-minded people can be about class. One of the functions of education should be to instil a healthy tolerance for all types of people. But often it does just the reverse. It is sometimes difficult to be tolerant without being patronizing. Here's an extract from *Eric, or Little by Little* by F. W. Farrar:

> **There was one point about Ayrton Latin School that [Eric] never regretted. It was the mixture there of all classes. On those benches gentlemen's sons sat side by side with plebeians, and no harm, but only good seemed to come from the intercourse...Many a time afterwards, when Eric, as he passed down the streets, interchanged friendly greetings with some young glazier or tradesman whom he remembered at school, he felt glad that thus early he had learnt practically to despise the accidental and nominal differences which separate man and man.**

It's important to have the right attitude to the lower orders, and particularly to servants. Here is a short poem which demonstrates a proper sense of priorities in such matters. It's a 'Ruthless Rhyme' by Harry Graham, entitled 'Mr Jones':

> **'There's been an accident,' they said.**
> **'Your servant's cut in half, he's dead!'**
> **'Indeed,' said Mr Jones, 'and please**
> **Send me the half that's got my keys.'**

It's no joke having servants (or so the tiny percentage of people in the country who have them keep assuring everyone else). The problems are immense. How do some people manage? Here's a letter from the correspondence columns of *The Times:*

> **But we cannot understand why, although there are thousands of women and girls unemployed, when we ask at the labour exchanges for domestic servants, we are told that none is available. I, for example, who live alone very quietly with a staff of seven domestics, am quite unable to obtain a kitchenmaid.**

It's inhuman that anyone should suffer such privations. And even if you are lucky enough to find staff, the behaviour of the serving classes can leave something to be desired, as in this report from the *Sunday Times:*

> **'Do you gents want something to drink?'**
> **Though said in a perfectly friendly manner, it was not, in my view, the right way for a wine waiter to address First Class passengers.**

Mind you, it is difficult to know what is correct behaviour at table. There are many issues of protocol raised even by a simple dinner party. If you have any problems in that area, it's probably advisable to consult an expert. Here's some useful information from *Housewife* magazine:

Nowadays, if you are worried about seating arrangements for your guests, you can write to the Heralds of the College of Arms and hope for a reply as superb as the one received by the anxious hostess of the Aga Khan. 'The Aga Khan,' it ran, 'is held by his followers to be the direct descendant of God. An English duke takes precedence.'

English dukes are an institution and the whole issue of hereditary honours provokes strong reactions from those of socialist views. Much of a person's social standing is determined simply by the accident of birth. Here's Thomas Hood on the subject, from his long poem, 'Miss Kilmansegg and Her Precious Leg':

> What different lots our stars accord!
> This babe to be hail'd and woo'd as a Lord!
>   And that to be shunn'd like a leper!
> One, to the world's wine, honey, and corn,
> Another, like Colchester native, born
>   To its vinegar, oil, and pepper.
>
> One is litter'd under a roof
> Neither wind nor water proof,—
>   That's the prose of Love in a Cottage,—
> A puny, naked, shivering wretch,
> The whole of whose birthright would not fetch,
> Though Robins himself drew up the sketch,
>   The bid of 'a mess of pottage'.
>
> Born of Fortunatus's kin,
> Another comes tenderly usher'd in
>   To a prospect all bright and burnish'd:
> No tenant he for life's back slums—
> He comes to the world as a gentleman comes
>   To a lodging ready furnish'd.

The survival of the British peerage is a living embodiment of the British class system. Here's Edmund Burke on the subject:

Nobility is a graceful ornament to the civil order. It is the Corinthian capital of polished society.

DUTY FIRST

Her Ladyship (who is giving a Servants' Ball) to Butler. 'We shall begin with a square dance, and I shall want you, Wilkins, to be my partner.'

Wilkins. 'Certainly, m'Lady; and afterwards I presoom we may dance with 'oom we like?'

The peers of the realm are born to rule, but perhaps not to cope with the more domestic details of life. Here's a report from the *Sunday Telegraph:*

The perils of travelling without a valet are illustrated by an experience which recently befell

the Duke of Marlborough as a guest of one of his daughters. She was surprised to hear him complain that his toothbrush 'did not foam properly', so would she buy him a new one. He had to be reminded gently that without the aid of toothpowder, usually applied for him each morning by his valet, no toothbrush foamed automatically.

It's very tempting to knock the aristocracy and it's a practice which has a long history. Here's the view of Matthew Arnold:

One has often wondered whether upon the whole earth there is anything so unintelligent, so unapt to perceive how the world is really going, as an ordinary young Englishman of our upper class.

Fond Parent (*who has done pretty well in woollens*). 'Well, Sonny, we've decided to give you the best education that money can buy. After all, you won't have to do anything except be a gentleman.'

At times it does seem that the upper classes are rather out of touch with real life. There's an air of fantasy surrounding the whole business of hereditary titles. A line from Oscar Wilde's *A Woman of No Importance*:

> **'You should study the Peerage, Gerald...It is the best thing in fiction the English have ever done.'**

At the top of the social ladder is the Royal Family, whose continuing presence ensures the preservation of the country's social fabric – a fact which is comforting or depressing according to your political convictions. The Royal Family, who manage one of the most difficult family businesses in the country with enormous efficiency, command tremendous loyalty. Many would still lay down their lives for them. Though sometimes the sacrifice required is less. From the *Sunday Express*:

> **At a two-roomed cottage near Glamis Castle, a white-haired mother spoke proudly yesterday of a little service she had been able to give the Royal Family. She revealed that 34 years ago she agreed to her baby son taking the birth registration number of 13, so that it should not go to Princess Margaret.**

That is what's called 'knowing one's place', and while such selflessness in social matters remains, the future of the British class system is assured.

-FOOD-

PRECEPT AND EXAMPLE.

A man went into a grocer's and saw a sign: 'Normal eggs 30p a dozen, square eggs 50p a dozen.' He asked the manager what the extra twenty pence was for.

'Ah,' came the reply, 'that's danger money for the chicken.'

'Waiter, waiter, what's in this stuff?'

'It's bean soup, sir.'

'I asked for its recipe, not its history.'

There was a Scottish baker who tried to economize by making the holes in his doughnuts bigger. He soon gave it up, though. The bigger the hole was the more dough he had to put round it.

'Waiter, waiter, this food isn't fit for a pig.'

'Very good sir. I'll go and get you some that is.'

'Waiter, waiter, do you have frogs' legs?'

'No, sir, I always walk this way.'

Mark two: 'Waiter, waiter, do you have frogs' legs?'

'Yes, sir.'

'Well, hop over the counter and get me a sandwich.'

'Waiter, waiter, there's a fly in my soup.'

'No, sir, actually that's the chef. The last customer was a witch doctor.'

'Waiter, waiter, this coffee tastes like tea.'

'Oh, I'm sorry, sir. I must have brought you cocoa by mistake.'

Mrs Cohen and Mrs Levy met in the street.

'Sssh,' said Mrs Cohen, 'don't tell a soul, but I'm having an affair.'

'Oh,' said Mrs Levy, 'and who's doing the catering?'

Diner. 'THIS COD ISN'T NEARLY SO NICE AS THAT I HAD A FEW DAYS AGO.'

Absent-minded Waiter. 'IT OUGHT TO BE, SIR; IT'S OFF THE VERY SAME FISH.'

Food is central to everyone's life, and there is a great deal of humour attached to the subject. Gluttons have always been thought funny; more recently the excesses of slimmers and dieters have found their way into comedy scripts; and the gastronomic differences between countries are still the most obvious means of identification for humorous purposes. The French are 'Frogs', the Germans are 'Krauts' – from Sauerkraut – the Irish are Murphys or spuds, and so on. Apparently it also works in reverse, and the French call us 'Rosbifs' – though that won't last long with current meat prices.

It has been held that personality is defined by diet – you are what you eat. Certainly Dr Johnson didn't think it a subject to be taken lightly:

> **Some people have a foolish way of not minding, or of pretending not to mind, what they eat. For my part, I mind my belly very studiously and very carefully; for I look upon it that he who does not mind his belly will hardly mind anything else.**

George Bernard Shaw wrote:

> **There is no love sincerer than the love of food.**

Guy de Maupassant was even more lyrical on the subject:

> **To be without a sense of taste is to be deficient in an exquisite faculty, that of appreciating the qualities of food, just as a person may lack the faculty of appreciating the quality of a book or a work of art. It is to want a vital sense, one of the elements of human superiority.**

Sydney Smith saw most of human behaviour in dietary terms:

Soup and fish explain half of the emotions of life.

And Mark Twain saw how food could enhance any pleasure:

Nothing helps scenery like ham and eggs.

And, while we're on eggs, let's hear from Oscar Wilde:

An egg is always an adventure; it may be different.

The trouble is, if an egg is too different, it can have nasty side-effects. Food poisoning is extremely unpleasant and not everyone shares the enviable insouciance of Mark Twain:

Part of the secret of success in life is to eat what you like and let the food fight it out inside.

But if you do have any trouble with your innards, keep cheerful about it. Here's an extract from a Cheshire Public Health Department circular:

The film reviews in a lively and amusing manner the various ways in which a victim of food poisoning might have been infected.

One sensible way of avoiding food poisoning is knowing who has prepared your food – or doing it yourself. There's nothing like home cooking. Hence, presumably, the enormous sales of cookery books. New ones seem to come out about three times a day with such trendy titles as *Geoffrey Chaucer's Middle English Cookbook, The Imbecile's Guide to Cookery, 1001 New Things to Do with an Aubergine, the Bedsit Stuffed Camel Recipe Book.* What is more, they are all bought and then join the vast pile of other cookery books on a greasy kitchen shelf. And then they're forgotten about. I should think, apart from one or two invaluable volumes, the average new cookbook is used by the average housewife about once.

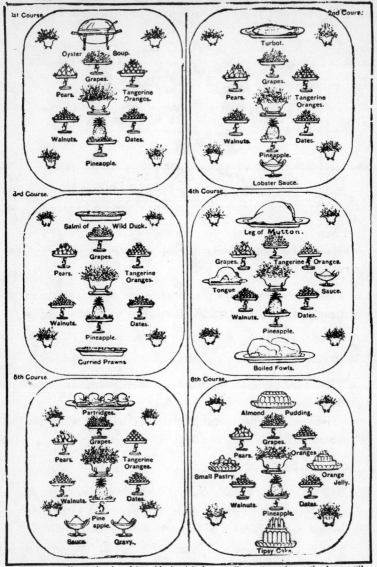

Note.—According to the size of the table, it might be as well to omit putting on the dessert till after the sixth course

But that's not the point. A new recipe can add a touch of the exotic to a mundane meal. Here's a notice from a Cheltenham food shop:

Cotswold Mushroom PIE
Genuine French Recipe

Let's have a few real recipes while we're on the subject. First, from a daily paper:

> **Take some eating pears, peel them, and cook them slowly standing in water flavoured with one vanilla pod.**

Question from the *US Army Times:*

> **'How can I give summer sweet potatoes more flavour?'**
> **– Try adding a tablespoonful of water to the water in which they are boiled.**

Or, from the *American Weekly:*

> **Peanut-butter grilled corn: Husk fresh corn; spread ears lightly with peanut butter. Wrap each ear with bacon slice; fasten with toothpick. Place on grill, turning until done – about ten minutes. Or let everyone grill his own ears, using long skewers to do so.**

To bake a Carp according to these Forms to be eaten hot.

Take a carp, scale it, and scrape off the slime, bone it, and cut it into dice-work, the milt being parboild, cut it into the same form, then have some great oysters parboild and cut in the same form also ; put to it some grapes, goosberries, or barberries, the bottoms of artichocks boild the yolks of hard eggs in quarters, boild sparagus cut an inch long, and some pistaches, season all the foresaid things together with pepper, nutmegs, and salt, fill the pyes, close them up, and bake them, being baked, liquor them with butter, white-wine, and some blood of the carp, boil them together, or beaten butter with juyce of oranges.

To bake a Carp with Eels to be eaten cold.

Take four large carps, scale them and wipe off the slime clean, bone them, and cut each side into two pieces of every carp, then have four large fresh water eels, fat ones, boned

SOYER'S SAUCE.
Sold only in the above bottles, holding half-a-pint.
PRICE 2s. 6d.

Fortunately, human ears in food are, since the demise of Sweeney Todd, a rarity. But let's move from such slightly unwholesome gastronomic thoughts to one of the greatest paeans of praise to any dish in the English language – Sydney Smith's 'Recipe for Salad':

To make this condiment, your poet begs
The pounded yellow of two hard-boiled eggs,
Two boiled potatoes, passed through kitchen-sieve,
Smoothness and softness to the salad give;
Let onion atoms lurk within the bowl,
And, scarce-suspected, animate the whole.
Of mordant mustard add a single spoon,
Distrust the condiment that bites so soon;
But deem it not, thou man of herbs, a fault,
To add a double quantity of salt.
And, lastly, o'er the flavoured compound toss
A magic soup-spoon of anchovy sauce.
Oh, green and glorious! Oh, herbaceous treat!
'Twould tempt the dying anchorite to eat;
Back to the world he'd turn his fleeting soul,
And plunge his fingers in the salad bowl!
Serenely full, the epicure would say,
Fate cannot harm me, I have dined today.

Salad features largely in many diets, since as yet there have been few scares about the dangers of fresh vegetables – almost every other food has at some stage been discredited. Also salads are very good for the calory-conscious. But diets are not just observed to combat obesity. They can do all kinds of things, though some people, like this enquirer to the magazine, *Health for All*, ask rather a lot of them:

> I am twenty-nine, single; I neither drink nor smoke.
> I do not seem to be able to overcome the sex
> impulse. Is this due to catarrh, and will a diet of
> vegetables and salads help to abate it?

People do take diets seriously and many – of both sexes – live their lives in a maze of books and wall-charts, their minds buzzing with sums and permutations of carbohydrate units at every meal. For them, the simple offer of a drink becomes a major problem of mathematics and morality. Here's an anonymous epitaph on a slimmer:

**All her life she waged war on
Her excess flesh – and now it's gone.**

EPISODE IN HIGH LIFE

The Lady Kerosine de Colza. 'I cannot tell you how pleased I am to meet you here, Dr Blenkinsop, and especially to go down to dinner with you.'

Dr Blenkinsop (an eminent Physician, much pleased). 'You flatter me, I'm sure, Lady Kerosine!'

Lady Kerosine. 'Oh, no! It's so nice to sit by somebody who can tell you what to eat, drink, and avoid, you know!'

Over the centuries, the main dietary advice that has been put forward is moderation. Here's what the Talmud says:

In eating, a third of the stomach should be filled with food, a third with drink, and the rest left empty.

74

Benjamin Franklin also attacked excess:

In general, mankind, since the improvement of cooking, eats twice as much as nature requires.

A VOLUPTUARY under the horrors of Digestion.

At the other end of the scale from the glutton or gourmand is the gourmet whose taste for well-cooked food is the reason why restaurants are so expensive. It actually seems that the more limited the menu is in a restaurant, the higher the prices are. Mind you, one hears worrying stories about even the top restaurants, in the matter of hygiene. And lower down the scale, you take your life in your own hands every time you go out to eat. Here's a report from the *Western Daily Press:*

> **Waitresses used eyebrow tweezers to remove flakes of rust in dishes of jelly at [the cafeteria]. And Councillor Will Johns, who told this story to the city council last night, asked that in future the eyebrow tweezers be sterilized.**

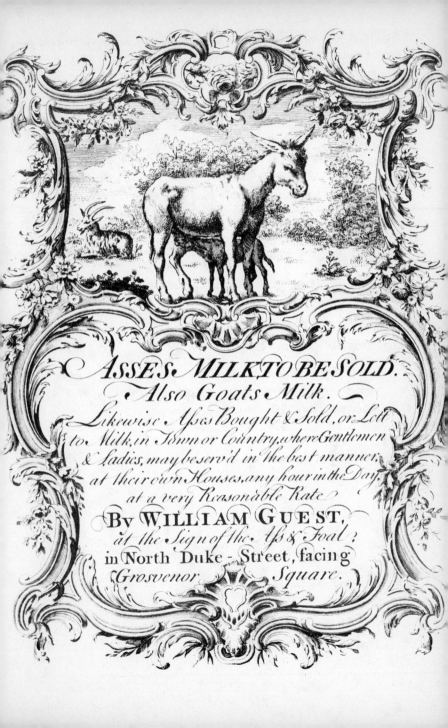

ASSES MILK TO BE SOLD.
Also Goats Milk.
Likewise Asses Bought & Sold, or Lett
to Milk, in Town or Country, where Gentlemen
& Ladies, may be serv'd in the best manner,
at their own Houses, any hour in the Day,
at a very Reasonable Rate

By WILLIAM GUEST,
at the Sign of the Ass & Foal,
in North Duke - Street, facing
Grosvenor Square.

Another newspaper report on an even lower form of gastronomy – school food. This one's from the *Daily Express:*

> **Corned beef was sent to a Bridgend school canteen. Teachers sniffed it and did not like it. A canteen manageress sniffed it but pronounced it good; the town sanitary inspector sniffed it, and passed it as good; the town medical officer sniffed it, and declared it good – then ordered it to be destroyed because too many people had sniffed it.**

But one mustn't be put off by such horror stories. Food is important to all of us and a good digestion is often a sign of more general well-being. Budd Schulberg:

> **The only times I could digest were when I was liking everybody around me.**

And a closing thought on the same lines from – rather appropriately – Charles Lamb:

> **Coleridge declares that a man cannot have a good conscience who refuses apple dumplings, and I confess I am of the same opinion.**

-PARTIES-

ST MADE A MESS OF IT, ALF. RAN INTO A LADY AND SUGGESTED TAKING MASKS OFF FOR FUN, YOU KNOW, AND SHE SAYS 'SIR! I'M NOT WEARING A MASK!'

A drunken man at a party went up to a strange woman and embraced her clumsily. She slapped his face.

'I'm so sorry,' he said, 'I thought you were my wife.'

'Huh,' said the woman, 'You'd be a fine husband to have. Just look at you — a drunken, clumsy, disgusting brute.'

'Good heavens,' said the drunk, 'you talk like her, too.'

A very fat man met a friend who also used to be fat, but was transformed into a little, trim figure. He'd lost two stone in a fortnight. 'How did you do it?' asked the fat one. 'Diet?'

'Partly,' said the trim one, 'but it's drugs mainly. I went to Dr Brown and he gave me these amazing tablets.'

'But don't they have unpleasant side-effects?'

'No,' said the other. 'They're very nice. Every night when I go to sleep, I dream I'm on a desert island with hundreds of native girls. I spend all my dreams chasing them round and when I wake up, I've lost another couple of pounds.'

'That's great,' said the fat man, and he rushed off to the doctor's surgery and got his prescription for the tablets and started taking them. But within a week he was back at the doctor's, thinner but disgruntled.

'What's the problem?' asked the doctor. 'You're losing weight.'

'Oh yes,' he replied, 'but my friend has this marvellous dream about chasing native girls. I dream I'm on a desert island, but it's full of ghastly cannibals, and they chase me all night.'

'It's quite simple,' Dr Brown explained. 'Your friend's a private patient; you are on the National Heatlh.'

An old man went to a fancy dress ball at a **Nudist Camp**. He won first prize as the **Dead Sea Scrolls**. He was furious — he'd gone as a prune.

'I went to a party last night and we played Jockey's Knock.'
  'What's that?'
  'It's like Postman's Knock, but with more horseplay.'

A man was walking past a building site when he was surprised to see three big Irish labourers holding hands and dancing round a hole in the ground.

  'What's up?' he asked the foreman. 'Is it someone's birthday?'

  'No,' said the foreman, 'it's the third anniversary of the hole.'

Ordinary people go to champagne parties; hypochondriacs go to sham pain parties.

A man came back from a party very drunk and just as he was creeping in by the front door he heard his wife moving upstairs. 'Oh – oh,' he thought, 'she mustn't think I've been drinking. I know, I'll pretend I've been reading all evening.'

So he put the plan into action, went into the sitting-room and sat down. After a few minutes the door opened and his wife peered in.

'What do you think you're doing?' she asked.

'Reading, dear, just reading.'

'Shut up, you drunken idiot,' said the wife. 'Now close that suitcase and come to bed.'

Everyone is a bit different at a party. There's another personality that takes over. People who are normally relaxed and chatty stiffen up into mouthing idiots, and shy, retiring types suddenly break out into noisy extroverts. It's partly the alcohol, but there's more to it than that.

There's something about parties. A lot of people claim to hate them – a lot *do* hate them, but this doesn't stop the haters from attending or feeling piqued when not invited. Oscar Wilde sums up this ambivalence to society in *A Woman of No Importance*. Gerald says:

'I suppose society is wonderfully delightful!'

And Lord Illingworth replies:

'To be in it is merely a bore. But to be out of it simply a tragedy.'

But people go on giving parties, in spite of disasters. Major events must be celebrated with a party. Weddings, for instance. A report from a Nebraska newspaper:

A reception immediately followed the ceremony with papers and flowers decorating the table, with the traditional tired wedding cake.

Or a tea-party, after a conference, say, like this one reported in a Devon paper:

A committee of ladies, with Mrs Roberts as leader, threw themselves into the tea, which proved a masterpiece.

That sort of semi-official party is fraught with problems in the planning stages. From the *Daily Mirror:*

> **Mr Curry, who is the Maidstone agent said: 'They were planning to call the get-together a cheese and wine party, until I pointed out to them that it was illegal. We didn't want to get into trouble so we changed the name. We thought if we called it "cheese and you know what"everyone would think of wine. It's rather unfortunate!'**

I suppose people go on giving parties, hoping for the final accolade of being thought a good host. Not everybody makes it. Max Beerbohm:

> **Macbeth and Lady Macbeth stand out as the supreme type of all that a host and hostess should not be.**

Some hosts cheat about parties. Rather than suffering all of the tribulations of arrangements themselves, they take their friends out to a restaurant to eat. This is an extremely expensive way of doing things and you have to be very careful in your choice of venue. You can't believe all the advertisements say. Or sometimes you can – and that's worse:

> **Come to Blank's Restaurant where good food is an unexpected pleasure.**

Or try this one:

> **At our restaurant parties up to 1,000 can and have been done.**

But, if you go to a restaurant, you do miss out on a lot of the fun of giving a party – all the organization – invitations, buying food and drink. Remember, a good party is a well-prepared party. Here's a very useful tip for party-givers from the *Caterham Times:*

If you are having dancing and don't want your carpet ruined, to save taking it up, turn it upside down.

Dancing may not be a good idea for a party. It can be aesthetically unattractive. Heinrich Heine:

British women dance as though they were riding on donkeys.

And dancing is a potential source of immorality. Here's a description of a particular lady by Sallust:

She could dance more skilfully than an honest woman need.

Dancing always provokes disapproval. An English diplomat in the '20s made this comment on first seeing the tango danced at a *thé dansant* in Paris:

> **Modern dancing is like a country walk slightly impeded by a member of the opposite sex.**

Dancing can also lead to all kinds of goings-on — perhaps not the sort of thing you want at your party. Some dances are worse than others. The disgusting erotic potential of the waltz shocked Lord Byron:

From where the garb just leaves the bosom free,
That spot where hearts were once supposed to be;
Round all the confines of the yielded waist,
The strangest hand may wander undisplaced;
The lady's in return may grasp as much
As princely paunches offer to her touch...
Thus front to front the partners move or stand,
The foot may rest, but none withdraw the hand.

But even without the overt immorality of dancing, parties still carry overtones of sex. Robert Surtees:

> **These sort of boobies think that people come to balls to do nothing but dance; whereas everyone knows that the real business of a ball is either to look out for a wife, to look after a wife, or to look after somebody else's wife.**

HINTS TO CLIMBERS: HOW TO ATTRACT NOTICE.
II. INVENT (IF POSSIBLE) A SILLIER AND MORE UNDIGNIFIED DANCE THAN HAS EVER BEEN DANCED BEFORE.

As well as providing attractive potential pick-ups, the good host should also offer a few 'interesting people' at his party. Social head-hunting is a popular game amongst party-givers. If you can produce a tame novelist, playwright, artist or footballer, then you are succeeding socially.

The idea is that the wit of the guests reflects well on the taste and intelligence of the host. However, this does not always work because it's a fallacy that famous people are infallibly interesting to listen to. Here's Sydney Smith on Lord Macaulay:

He has occasional flashes of silence that make his conversation perfectly delightful.

On the other hand, given the right build-up, someone with a reputation for repartee can get away with murder. Here's a line by W. S. Gilbert from *The Yeomen of the Guard:*

'Tis ever thus with simple folk – an accepted wit has but to say 'Pass the mustard' – and they roar their ribs out.

But take care when inviting the famous to your party that they think it worthwhile. If they don't, they can turn their wit against their host – and destroy all his social planning. Dr Johnson, after an evening out:

This was a good dinner enough, to be sure; but it was not a dinner to *ask* a man to.

The more formal a party, the more essential it is for the guests to behave correctly. Here are a few useful tips, first from a Sunday paper:

Be very careful about nakedness at a cocktail party. It is not really the place.

Next, an enquiry from the *Daily Mirror:*

'Will you please tell me the correct way to eat grapes?'

– I have always eaten grapes by picking the fruit from the stem, conveying them to my mouth with my fingers, and removing pips by ejecting them into the hollow of my hands.

And, finally, from a book of etiquette:

It is not considered polite to tear bits off your beard and put them in your soup.

All useful information. Another problem for the host at a party is conversation. He has to ensure that people circulate and talk to each other; above all, that they are kept interested. And it's difficult. Lord Byron again:

Society is now one polish'd horde,
Formed of two mighty tribes – the *Bores* and *Bored*.

If you're not careful you can end up with a disaster on your hands, the sort of social event described by P. G. Wodehouse:

It was one of those parties where you cough twice before you speak and then decide not to say it after all.

Maybe the best thing to do is to keep the drink flowing and hope that all your guests are nice, friendly people. And, if we are to believe this report by James Boswell, don't invite Dr Johnson:

The Abbé Reynal probably remembers that, being at the house of a common friend in London, the master of it approached Johnson with that gentleman so much celebrated in his hand, and this speech in his mouth: 'Will you permit me, Sir, to present to you the Abbé Reynal?' 'No, Sir,' replied the Doctor very loud, and suddenly turned away from them both.

And now here's a description of a party given by Charles and Carrie Pooter, taken from the immortal *Diary of a Nobody* by George and Weedon Grossmith:

November 15: A red-letter day. Our first important party since we have been in this house. I got home early from the City. My son, Lupin, insisted on having a hired waiter, and stood a half-dozen of champagne. I think this an unnecessary expense, but Lupin said he had had a piece of luck, having made three pounds out of a private deal in the City. I hope he won't gamble in his new situation. The supper-room looked so nice, and Carrie truly said: 'We need not be ashamed of its being seen by Mr Perkupp, your principal, should he honour us by coming.'

I dressed early in case people should arrive punctually at eight o'clock, and was much vexed to find my new dress-trousers much too short. Lupin, who is getting beyond his position, found fault with my wearing ordinary boots instead of dress-boots.

I replied satirically: 'My dear son, I have lived to be above that sort of thing.'

Lupin burst out laughing, and said: 'A man generally was above his boots.'

This may be funny, or it may *not*; but I was gratified to find he had not discovered the coral had come off one of my studs. Carrie looked a picture, wearing the dress she wore at the Mansion House.

The arrangement of the drawing-room was excellent. Carrie had hung muslin curtains over the folding-doors, and also over one of the entrances, for we had removed the door from its hinges.

Mr Peters, the waiter, arrived in good time, and I gave him strict orders not to open another bottle of champagne until the previous one was empty. Carrie arranged for some sherry and port wine to be placed on the drawing-room sideboard, with some glasses. By-the-by, our new enlarged and tinted photographs look very nice on the walls, especially as Carrie has arranged some Liberty silk bows on the four corners of them.

The first arrival was Gowing, who, with his usual taste, greeted me with 'Hulloh, Pooter, why, your trousers are too short!'

I simply said: 'Very likely, and you will find my temper "short" also.'

He said: 'That won't make your trousers longer, Juggins. You should get your missus to put a flounce on them.'

I wonder I waste my time entering his insulting observations in my diary.

The next arrivals were Mr and Mrs Cummings. The former said: 'As you didn't say anything about dress, I have come "half-dress".' He had on a black frock-coat and white tie. The Jameses, Mr Merton, and Mr Stillbrook arrived, but Lupin was restless and unbearable till his Daisy Mutlar and Frank arrived. Carrie and I were rather startled at Daisy's appearance. She had a bright crimson dress on, cut very low in the the neck. I do not think such a style modest. She ought to have taken a lesson from Carrie, and covered her shoulders with a little lace. Mr Nackles, Mr Sprice-Hogg and his four daughters came; so did Franching, and one or two of Lupin's new friends, members of the 'Holloway

Comedians'. Some of these seemed rather theatrical in their manner, especially one, who was posing all the evening, and leant on our little round table and cracked it.

We had some music, and Lupin, who never left Daisy's side for a moment, raved over her singing of a song called 'Some Day'. It seemed a pretty song, but she made such grimaces, and sang, to my mind, so out of tune, I would not have asked her to sing again; but Lupin made her sing four songs right off, one after the other.

At ten o'clock we went down to supper, and from the way Gowing and Cummings ate you would have thought they had not had a meal for a month. I told Carrie to keep something back in case Mr Perkupp should come by mere chance.

Gowing annoyed me very much by filling a large tumbler of champagne, and drinking it straight off. He repeated this action, and made me fear our half-dozen of champagne would not last out. I tried to keep a bottle back, but Lupin got hold of it, and took it to the side-table with Daisy and Frank Mutlar.

We went upstairs, and the young fellows began skylarking. Carrie put a stop to that at once. Stillbrook amused us with a song, 'What have you done with your Cousin John?' I did not notice that Lupin and Frank had disappeared. I asked Mr Watson, one of the Holloways, where they were, and he said: 'It's a case of, "Oh, what a surprise!".'

We were directed to form a circle – which we did. Watson then said: 'I have much pleasure in introducing the celebrated Blondin Donkey.' Frank and Lupin then bounded into the room. Lupin had whitened his face like a clown, and Frank had tied round his waist a large hearthrug. He was supposed to be the donkey, and he looked it. They indulged in a very noisy pantomime, and we were all shrieking with laughter.

I turned round suddenly, and then I saw Mr Perkupp standing half-way in the door, he having arrived without our knowing it. I beckoned to Carrie, and we went up to him at once. He would not come right into the room. I apologised for the foolery, but Mr Perkupp said: 'Oh, it seems amusing.' I could see he was not a bit amused.

Carrie and I took him downstairs, but the table was a wreck. There was not even a glass of champagne left – not even a sandwich. Mr Perkupp said he required nothing, but would like a glass of seltzer or soda water. The last syphon was empty. Carrie said: 'We have plenty of port wine left.' Mr Perkupp said with a smile: 'No, thank you. I really require nothing, but I am most pleased to see you and your husband in your own home. Good-night, Mrs Pooter – you will excuse my very short stay, I know.' I went with him to his carriage, and he said: 'Don't trouble to come to the office till twelve tomorrow.'

I felt despondent as I went back to the house, and I told Carrie I thought the party was a failure. Carrie said it was a great success, and I was only tired, and insisted on my having some port myself. I drank two glasses, and felt much better, and went into the drawing-room, where they had commenced dancing. Carrie and I had a little dance, which I said reminded me of old days. She said I was a spooney old thing.

Harassed Hostess. 'Do you dance, or are you a walnut ?'

And I'm afraid that the next entry records that Charles Pooter had a rather bad hangover. That's the trouble with all parties. Lord Byron again:

Let us have wine and women, mirth and laughter,
Sermons and soda-water the day after.

Yes, eat, drink and be merry, for tomorrow you'll feel like death. And it's not just the physical disorder; there's the ghastly self-recrimination as you remember little details of your behaviour. This closing thought from Logan Pearsall Smith echoes something we have all thought at times:

The servant gave me my coat and hat, and in a glow of self-satisfaction I walked out into the night. 'A delightful evening,' I reflected, 'the nicest kind of people. What I said about finance and French philosophy impressed them; and how they laughed when I imitated a pig squealing.'

But soon after, 'God, it's awful,' I muttered, 'I wish I were dead.'

—HOBBIES—

A connoisseur was showing a friend his collection. 'Come this way. Look, I must show you this. It's the pride of my collection – a globe of sixteenth-century manufacture. It's in gold, you see, with the countries picked out in diamonds, and the trade routes picked out in silver. What do you think?'

'Incredible. Is it genuine?' asked his friend.

'Well, if it isn't, I was done for two quid,' came the reply.

'What do you call a person who collects money?'

'A numismatist.'

'No, you fool, it's a rent man.'

A fisherman invited a friend round for a rather special meal and couldn't resist boasting about the main course. 'Do you know,' he said, 'I fought for an hour with that salmon?'

'Yes,' said his friend, 'why somebody can't design an efficient tin-opener, I don't know.'

'Tell me, why did you take up gardening?'

'I was looking for digs.'

APT NOMENCLATURE IN OUR GARDEN SUBURB.

'Tell me about this hobby of yours — parachuting. When did you first take it up?'

'The day my plane caught fire.'

An Irishman took a photograph of his son to the chemist. 'I wonder,' he said, 'could you enlarge this for me?'

'Yes, certainly,' the chemist replied.

'And would it be possible for you to take his hat off for me?'

'Well, I'm sure we could do something. Yes, we could touch it up for you.'

'Oh, that's fine.'

'Tell me,' said the chemist, 'which side does your son part his hair?'

The Irishman smiled. 'Oh, come on now. You'll see that when you take his hat off.'

Two rather simple types hired a boat at the seaside one day and went fishing. They had very good luck and caught lots of fish. 'This is a good place,' said one. 'It'd be good to have another go tomorrow, but we'll never find it again.'

'Don't worry,' said the other, 'I've marked the side of the boat with a cross.'

'That's no good. We may not get the same boat tomorrow.'

The trouble with investigating the humour of hobbies is that, however you approach it, you are bound to leave a lot of them out. There are so many hobbies and each one is all-important to its devotees. So I must apologize if your particular fancy is not mentioned in this chapter. Bad luck, cigarette card collectors; bad luck, traction engine spotters, manhole cover fanatics and all of you who are currently making matchstick models of Liverpool Street Station.

Actually, those whose hobbies are not mentioned may be glad of it. Because a hobby is a consuming passion and, for some, even to look for humour in their passion is sacrilege. A hobby is a very personal thing. The derivation of the word is interesting. It comes from hobby-horse, and riding a hobby-horse is something which involves no one else. Laurence Sterne:

So long as a man rides his hobby-horse peaceably and quietly along the king's highway, and neither compels you or me to get up behind him, – pray, Sir, what have either you or I to do with it?

Yes, it's a private bee in the bonnet, a hobby. And very popular. Sir Matthew Hale in the seventeenth century:

Almost every person hath some hobby-horse or other.

It's a fancy that must be indulged. Sir Walter Scott:

I quarrel with no man's hobby.

And its obsessive force is something that is peculiarly English. George Santayana:

England is the paradise of individuality, eccentricity, heresy, anomalies, hobbies and humours.

People need hobbies to broaden their horizons, to make them feel that life is not just a continual round of work. A hobby opens another window on life. And having another outlet can help in one's main work. Ben Jonson:

Ease and relaxation are profitable to all studies. The mind is like a bow, the stronger by being unbent.

It's important to unbend – and not just for gardeners and deep-sea divers. For some people, a hobby begins as a conscious effort. Reading the first book on the subject is done with diffidence; it's after that the obsession builds. Collectors begin in an amateur way, before they become afficionados. This is certainly true of antique dealers. Many of them start off as amateurs. But then the hobby becomes a profession. The advantage of this is that when you give up the profession, you can keep the hobby. Here's a Freudian misprint from a newspaper's gossip column:

I did not see Mr M at the Antique Dealers' Fair last week, and later I heard that he has retired from the business and is faking things quietly at home.

Collecting can be a rather passive business, though, and there are a lot of people who prefer to burn up their leisure hours in more active pursuits. For many a hobby is a chance to take on another role – to do on an amateur level what others do professionally. This is certainly true of amateur dramatics enthusiasts and amateur musicians. They have all the excitement of the real thing without the pressures of careers depending on it. And they get the thrill of Press cuttings from local papers to cherish in their scrapbooks. Cuttings like these:

Mr Wilkinson's performance as the Prince never let us forget what a difficult play *Hamlet* **is.**

In the banquet scene, Emily Pritchett, as Lady Macbeth, really made a meal of the role.

Ibsen's play is finely balanced on a knife-edge between comedy and tragedy but the Walton Young Players managed to pull it off.

And then there's music. From a Surrey paper:

Miss Mary Salter rendered three vocal solos and a return to orchestral music was greatly appreciated.

Or from a Lincolnshire one:

Miss Tompkins is again the honorary conductor, and so long as this popular and talented lady holds the reins of the Choral Society there need be no fear of success.

The trouble with that kind of club or society hobby is that it tends to get bogged down in all kinds of administrative wrangles, all the little points of management that are dealt with by the inevitable committee. Committees do not always seem to be the most efficient methods of managing things and there is a lot of truth in the old definition of a camel as 'a horse designed by a committee'. Also committees are always in danger of being taken over by committee types, people who actually get pleasure from all the minutiae of signing minutes, making points of order and talking through the Chair.

But although all that committee business can be infuriating, committees do actually make important decisions for the societies which they control. A report from the old *News Chronicle:*

FIRST NIGHT OF AN UNAPPRECIATED
MELODRAMA

He. 'Are we alone?'
Voice from the Gallery: 'No, Guv'nor; but you will be to-morrow night.

103

Women in the Essex Village of Ugley have changed the name of their organization from the Ugley Women's Institute to the Women's Institute (Ugley Branch).

Societies like the Women's Institutes are very useful centres for hobbies – flower-arranging, cookery, needlework and other pursuits, as revealed in the Stourbridge edition of the *County Express:*

In the handicrafts exhibition at Wordsley Community Centre, the contribution of the Misses Smith was 'smocking and rugs' and not 'smoking drugs' as stated in last week's report.

Some hobbies can be indulged by members of both sexes but a lot are restricted to one or other. Obsessive interest in forms of transport is, on the whole, a masculine hobby. Kenneth Grahame's Mr Toad is a good example of this sort of enthusiast with his wild crazes, first to own a caravan and then a car. This kind of character always wants the latest in locomotion. It's very nice for those who have the money to indulge whims of this sort. Take Hilaire Belloc's 'Lord High-Bo':

> **Lord High-Bo, getting tired of trains,**
> **Would binge about in Aero-planes,**
> **A habit which would not have got**
> **Him into trouble, had he not**
> **Neglected what we know to be**
> **The rule of common courtesy.**
> **Past bedroom windows he would sail**
> **And with a most offensive hail**
> **Disturb the privacy of those**
> **About to wash or change their clothes.**

People whose finances don't run to aeroplanes can get the same kind of satisfaction from cars. Tinkering with engines and toolboxes and jacks and spanners is a totally obsessive hobby. Its adherents fall into two groups: those who work endlessly in garages rebuilding ancient motors they respect too much ever to use; and those who can't wait to get on the roads in an old banger tarted up with a positive acne of spotlamps, a ten-foot radio aerial and a chequered strip along the bottom of the door bearing the car's make, for passers-by who can't recognize the model under its layers of matt paint and chrome. For both these enthusiasts the car is everything. They spend all their money on accessories and tools, and all the time they are not actually under the car is devoted to searching motoring magazines for the latest knick-knack – for instance:

Something New Which No Motorist Should Be Without. We offer you THE SELF-GRIP WENCH.

It is possible to have a useful hobby, something that does a bit of good while it entertains you. Gardening's a good example of this. Though it remains a terrible chore for many, the real fanatic can spend all his time at it. Like most majority hobbies, it's very well documented. There are lots of books, magazines and catalogues around. There's a chance for enthusiasts to discuss methods through the Press. Here's a testimonial from a seedsman's catalogue:

I am very pleased with the lot of seeds I got from you recently. Every one nearly came up.

Tramp (mistaking garden suburb householder for one of his own profession).
'You're wasting your time, Charlie. The last time I clipped that 'edge I was rewarded with three 'a' pence, a cup o' tea nearly warm and a pair o' cycling knickers I wouldn't be seen dead in.'

And an interesting gardening story from a letter in *The People:*

At a neighbour's suggestion I tied old sacking around the base of my apple tree to trap insects. The first time I moved it I found hundreds of earwigs. Just as I was about to destroy them I remembered reading that earwigs are devoted mothers, risking anything to protect their young. I replaced the sacking without killing one. Needless to say there isn't an apple fit to eat.

That kind of sensibility isn't shared by devotees of another popular hobby, fishing. This is really the classic hobby, totally introverted, totally absorbing to those who like it, and totally pointless to those who don't. There's really no argument about fishing, since there is absolutely no common ground between those who like it and those who hate it. There have been critics. Dr Johnson:

A fishing rod is a stick with a hook at one end and a fool at the other.

Don Marquis:

Fishing is a delusion entirely surrounded by liars in old clothes.

But the fisherman is unaffected by that sort of talk. His eyes can only see his float, while his mind reaches out to a monster pike, a giant salmon or dreams the impossible bream. Success or failure doesn't matter; the possibility of a record-breaking fish is always there. The fisherman angles on, impervious to rational arguments, like this one from Mark Twain:

There is no use in walking five miles to fish when you can depend on being just as unsuccessful near home.

Fishing is another well-documented hobby. There are lots of papers and magazines full of photographs of chaps holding up fish. And there are reports on the angling scene. From an Aldershot paper:

I saw him land at least five big dace and roach. They expressed their admiration of the water, and of the Farnham Angling Society.

Or, from the *Angler's News:*

During the morning I wandered round the lake taking photographs and while doing this fell in with Mr L. R. Singer, who was fishing. A discussion on tactics ensued.

Fishing has its own language. Two anglers can converse for hours about multipliers, swim-feeders, paternosters, snap-tackle and swing-tips and leave the layman dazed and bewildered. This sort of thing gives fellow enthusiasts a snobbish exclusivity.

It's the same with any hobby. If you know about it, you are one of the 'in' crowd. Hi-fi is a good example of this, where the technicalities become daily more complex and the enthusiasts daily less comprehensible. Of course, as everyone knows, the attraction of hi-fi is not playing and listening to records and tapes. That's a by-product; what appeals is fiddling about with all those little bits of equipment.

Listening to records is a fairly passive form of hobby, but many surveys have shown that the most popular leisure activity in this country is even more passive. It's watching television.

Perhaps that's a depressing comment on our society, that with all the other more energetic or mentally stimulating leisure activities

Exhilarated Visitor (leaving Club). 'The feller who caught that fish 's dem liar.'

---

that are available, most people still prefer the sedentary pleasure of being effortlessly entertained. But, before you get too gloomy about the fraying moral fibre of this country, I'll cheer you up with a splendid example of British initiative. Television addicts, take note of this letter sent by a lady to the *Daily Herald:*

I do not like wasting time when I watch TV on my own. I like to do something else at the same time. I do foot, finger and eye exercises. I shrug my shoulders and roll my head round and round. During the Wimbledon Tournament, whenever the players changed ends I went down on my back to do a few tummy exercises and circled my legs round in the air.

So, even if your hobby is nothing more than watching television, there's no need to lose ambition. Because most people with a hobby have ambitions within the scope of that hobby. The ambitions are secret and personal, as secret and personal as the hobby itself. And sometimes the ambitions can have disastrous consequences. I'll close with a tragic epitaph by J. B. Morton:

A glassblower lies here at rest
Who one day burst his noble chest
While trying, in a fit of malice,
To blow a second Crystal Palace.

– SPORTS –

EFFETS ET POSES
Une balle qui n'est pas perdue pour tout le monde

'Do you know, George, I got a set of golf clubs for my wife last week.'

'Oh, Lionel, what a bargain.'

A football fan took his new girlfriend to a match for the first time, and answered all her questions as she inquired about the function of every player.

'And what's that man in the net?' she asked.

'He's the goal-keeper.'

'And what does he do?'

'He has to keep the ball from going in the net.'

'Ah. And how much is he paid?'

'Oh, about a hundred pounds a week.'

'Oh,' said the girl, 'wouldn't it be cheaper to board it up?'

A man and his wife were watching golf on the television and the sound on the commentary was rather low. The woman went to turn it up. 'Ssh,' said the husband, 'ssh. Not while he's putting.'

A famous footballer went to Heaven and was met by St Peter at the Pearly Gates. 'Who are you?' asked the saint. 'What did you do on earth?'

'I was a footballer.'

'Oh, and where are your boots?'

'I left them on earth.'

'Well, hurry back and get them — we're playing Hell tonight.'

The whole family was grouped round the television watching an international rugby match and the English full-back once again failed to intercept the opposing wing, who streaked home for his twentieth try.

'That full-back,' said the father, 'he's useless. I don't know why they let him play for the side at all.'

'Well,' said his five-year-old son, 'perhaps it's his ball.'

'Good morning, doctor.'

'Good morning. What's the trouble?'

'It's my shins, doctor. Look.'

'Good heavens. They're all hacked to pieces. Looks as if everyone's been kicking you. What have you been playing — soccer or rugby?'

'Bridge.'

There's a man playing golf and his caddie spends ages finding him the right club.

'Oh, come on, man. You must be the worst caddie on earth.'

'I doubt it,' the caddie says, 'that would be too much of a coincidence.'

Two flies were playing football in a saucer. One said to the other, 'Have to do better than this. Come on, we're playing in the cup next week.'

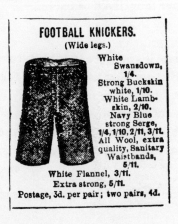

FOOTBALL KNICKERS.
(Wide legs.)

White Swansdown, 1/4. Strong Buckskin white, 1/10. White Lambskin, 2/10. Navy Blue strong Serge, 1/4, 1/10, 2/11, 3/11. All Wool, extra quality, Sanitary Waistbands, 5/11.

White Flannel, 3/11.
Extra strong, 5/11.
Postage, 3d. per pair; two pairs, 4d.

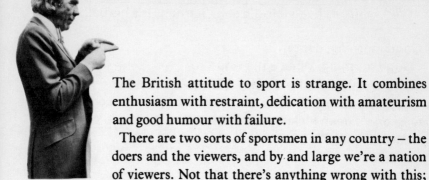

The British attitude to sport is strange. It combines enthusiasm with restraint, dedication with amateurism and good humour with failure.

There are two sorts of sportsmen in any country – the doers and the viewers, and by and large we're a nation of viewers. Not that there's anything wrong with this; a lot of notable thinkers have recommended keeping well clear of active sports. Dr Johnson, reported by Boswell:

Of common sports he once pleasantly remarked to me, How wonderfully well he continued to be idle without them.

George Santayana:

The need of exercise is a modern superstition, invented by people who ate too much, and had nothing to think about. Athletics don't make anybody either long-lived or useful.

Stephen Leacock:

As for exercise, if you have to take it, take it and put up with it. But as long as you have the price of a hack and can hire other people to play baseball for you and run races and do gymnastics when you sit in the shade and smoke and watch them – great heavens, what more do you want?

Thomas Tegg's *A Present for an Apprentice*, a book for children published in 1848, comes out more strongly against sport:

It is a general truth that those persons who are good at games are good at nothing else. Generally speaking, good players are but miserable and useless persons.

And yet, in spite of the body of opinion against sport, almost everyone must admit to a slight interest in some branch of it. Even Oscar Wilde:

I am afraid I play no outdoor games at all, except dominoes. I have sometimes played dominoes outside French cafés.

And there is a school of thought which still maintains the beneficial results of sporting activity. A view expressed by Benjamin Franklin:

Games lubricate the body and the mind.

What distinguishes the British attitude to sport from that of other countries is our view of the result. Thomas Fuller wrote in the sixteenth century:

It's a silly game where nobody wins.

The British would agree with that, but the British don't mind who wins. In fact, we rather enjoy losing. Here's a report from a leader in the *Evening News:*

No one in England will be peevish at the passing of the Ashes. We have been beaten by a much better team. Oddly enough, and to the permanent bewilderment of foreigners, this is an experience in which Englishmen still find a keen enjoyment.

Yes, all the world loves a loser and this is something that Britain is very good at producing. All that is required is for another of our white hopes in international contests to be trounced and immediately the sporting press burst into eulogies of his or her efforts, reports full of such words as 'tough', 'plucky', and 'game'. It is not thought 'quite nice' to win. Sport should be a genteel pastime for gentlemen.

It's not just lack of money that keeps so much British sport amateur; it's something in the national character as well. And this is expressed in cricket, our national game. Thomas Hughes dignifies cricket in *Tom Brown's Schooldays* with this description:

It's more than a game. It's an institution.

You see, cricket is a profoundly serious business and an interest in it must override all other considerations. A report from the *Sunday Times:*

The parson of a village where a friend of mine lives was perturbed at the persistent shortage of rain. Cattle and roots were suffering; the outlook was gloomy. He decided to pray for rain at morning service the next Sunday. Then a troublesome thought struck him. 'No,' he told my friend, 'not next Sunday; I shall put it off till the Sunday after. *I'm not going to do anything to spoil the Test Match.'*

And the institution of cricket is more than just a recreation; it's a training for the matches to be played on the great pitch of life. From the *Sunday Referee:*

King George of Greece was once bowled first ball in a cricket match at his English private school. He

never forgot the incident. It helped him, he said, to face the poverty-stricken years of his exile with more courage than he might otherwise have shown. It enabled him, he told friends, to treat the misfortune of his expulsion from Greece as a stepping stone to ultimate triumph.

Here's a remark from the MCC Secretary during the last war, quoted in the *Manchester Guardian:*

> Had Hitler and Mussolini been cricketers, I do not think we should have had all this trouble that is going on in Europe today.

Gretel. "HAVE YOU EVER CONTEMPLATED WHAT WOULD HAPPEN TO US ALL SHOULD THE ENEMY TRIUMPH?"
Hansel. "DON'T, GRETEL—DON'T! FANCY BEING FORCED TO PLAY CRICKET!"

Before we leave cricket, let's just hear one dissenting voice – Oscar Wilde:

> I do not play cricket, because it requires me to asssume such indecent postures.

And then of course there's football. In this sport professionalism has taken over the game and players change hands at enormous prices. Unlike cricket, football is a rather rough game, which has been condemned as violent for some centuries. Here's Sir Thomas Elyot, writing in 1531:

> **Football is nothyng but beastely fury and extreme violence, whereof procedeth hurte, and consequently rancour and malice do remayne with thym that be wounded, wherefore it is to be put in perpetuall silence.**

And Richard Melcaster, fifty years later:

> **The Footeball...as it is now commonly used, with thronging of a rude multitude, with bursting of shinnes, and breaking of legges, be neither civill, neither worthy the name of any traine to health.**

Things don't seem to have changed much in three hundred years. And what Oscar Wilde said on the subject is also still true:

> **Football is all very well as a game for rough girls, but it is hardly suitable for delicate boys.**

Enormous space in the press is devoted to football. The game is analyzed and dissected in prose that varies between purple extravagance and sheer incompetence. Here's a match report from a Kent paper:

> **The forwards shot hard and often but never straight till at last Hill decided to try his head. It came off first time.**

One of the most popular participant sports in this country is golf. Its devotees have no room in their minds for any other thoughts than those of the game. Here's Robert Lynd on the subject:

It is almost impossible to remember how tragic a place the world is when one is playing golf.

An alternative view was expressed by Mark Twain, who reckoned that a game of golf spoils a good walk. But such a thought is sacrilege to the golfing fanatic, to whom family, expense and inconvenience are no consideration. Here's an extract from an interview with one such, published in an evening paper:

I have been all over the world looking for the perfect golf curse, but I think at last I have found it.

A golfing enthusiast will play whenever possible. Even in wartime. In fact, new rules for the game were developed for special wartime situations. Here's one:

A ball moved by enemy action may be replaced as near as possible where it lay, or if lost or destroyed a ball may be dropped not nearer the hole without penalty.

There's a useful bit of information. Fortunately nowadays the specialized needs of golfers are being increasingly recognized. A report from the *Sunday Mirror:*

Every room in a £687,000 motel-cum-leisure centre to be built at Southport, Lancs, will be carpeted with artificial turf so golfing guests can practise putting in privacy.

Before we leave golf, it should be mentioned that it's a game of very strict etiquette, off the course as much as on. Club houses have a lot of rules:

For two hours the committee of a golf club in south-east England debated whether women players might be allowed to wear trousers on the links.

Their decision was: 'Trousers may be worn by women golfers on the course, but must be taken off on entering the club house.'

THE RULING PASSION

First Enthusiastic Golfer. 'I say, will you play another round with me on Thursday?'

Second Enthusiastic Golfer. 'Well, I'm booked to be married on that day—*but it can be postponed*!'

There are so many sports, all with their own humour, that it's going to be impossible to fit them all into this chapter. But here's a quick look at a couple of others. First, boxing. A report from the *Daily Express*:

The Bible is the inspiration of Joe Louis. He always reads it before entering the ring, and then, according to one of his seconds: 'All fortified and everything, he just wades in and knocks the other guy's block off.'

Athletics: from the *Yorkshire Evening Post:*

It was revealed today that G. L. Rampling, who won the quarter mile for England in the British Empire Games in 48 seconds, actually ran a greater distance. For the purposes of the record, the track at the White City, London, has been surveyed, and a certificate has been given stating that Rampling actually ran 440 yards three inches. This, of course, makes Rampling's feat all the more meritorious.

Most people in this country get no closer to sport than a television's distance away. We're a nation of armchair experts, who can see the right thing to do in our sitting-rooms with a clarity that the players on the field seem to lack. In the words of G. J. Renier:

It seems to me that the main contact of the bulk of English with sport consists in looking on and betting.

But for the real active sports enthusiast, there is no substitute. Sporting achievements are a great focus for dreams. I'll conclude with the view of a real fanatic – Robert Surtees's character Jorrocks on his great love – hunting:

'Unting fills my thoughts by day, and many a good run I have in my sleep. Many a dig in the ribs I gives Mrs J. when I think they're running into the warmint...No man fit to be called a sportsman wot doesn't kick his wife out of bed on a haverage once in three weeks!

-PETS-

I used to have a fish as a pet. Poor little thing – it was deaf. So I bought it a herring aid.

'Do you know what happened when I washed my hamster in detergent?'
  'No.'
  'It died.'
  'I'm not surprised. I could have told you detergent wasn't good for hamsters.'
  'It wasn't the detergent that killed it. It was the spin-drier.'

'Do you know, every day my dog and I go for a tramp in the woods.'
  'Oh, does the dog like that?'
  'Yes, but the tramp's getting a bit fed up with it.'

A flea went into a pub and ordered a double scotch. And another. And another. And another. He drank them all down and at closing time, he hopped unsteadily out into the street, then leapt in the air and fell flat on his face. 'Oh damn,' he said, 'someone's moved my dog.'

There was a bloke who   d £500 for a talking dog and took it home to show off to his friend. 'Look at this,' he said, 'a dog that talks.'
  'Ah, come off it,' said his friend. 'I'll offer you ten to one it doesn't say a word.'
  'Right,' said the owner, and told the dog to talk. Nothing. He wheedled, threatened, cajoled. Nothing. His friend roared with laughter, pocketed his winnings and left.
  The owner turned on the dog furiously. 'Why didn't you say something, you stupid animal?'
  'Not so much of the stupid,' said the dog. 'Just think of the odds you'll get next time.'

Two cats met in the street. 'Meow,' said the first cat.

'Woof,' said the second cat.

The first one tried again. 'Meow.'

'Woof,' said the second cat.

'Cats don't say "Woof",' said the first one.

'Sorry,' said the other. 'I'm a stranger around here.'

An old lady was very proud of her well-behaved parrot and was showing him off to the vicar. 'And he talks, you know. But none of those rude things that parrots usually say. He's very religious. If you pull his right leg, he recites the Lord's Prayer and if you pull his left leg, he recites the Twenty-Third Psalm.'

'That's remarkable,' said the vicar, 'quite remarkable. And what happens if you pull both legs at once?'

'I fall flat on my back, you stupid old twit,' said the parrot.

The British attitude to pets is a frequent source of humour, particularly for foreigners. Here's J. W. von Archenholz, writing in 1785:

> **In England animals are treated with almost as much humanity as though they were rational beings.**

It is also maintained that the British actually find it easier to communicate with animals than with people. Emily Hahn:

> **If it were not for his four-footed friends, many an Englishman would burst with suppressed emotion.**

Some people are quite frank about the situation. Here's a letter published in the *Daily Express:*

> **I personally own a bull terrier, and would say here and now that I have far more in common with my dog and any horse than I have with 99¾ per cent of the people I meet.**

The feeling for animals runs very strong in this country. There's no surer way for a writer or broadcaster to be inundated with irate letters than for him to say anything against pets. There are even occasional complaints that animals aren't catered for by the media. There are programmes *about* pets, but not many *for* pets. This hasn't always been so. Here's a report from the *News Chronicle:*

> **A special corner by dogs for dogs will be included in 'Calling All Dogs', which the BBC are putting on next Sunday in honour of 'Eve of Dog-Licence Day'. The view at Broadcasting House is that, although**

dogs do not normally display much interest in the loudspeaker, they will if special material is broadcast for them.

I think England is the only country where a programme for pets would even be considered.

Sometimes it seems there's a definite confusion of values in British attitudes to animals as against people. Results of charity appeals from a *Radio Times* of some years back:

East Islington Mothers' and Babies' Welfare Centre – £49. 10s. 8d.
People's Dispensary for Animals of the Poor – £11,812. 0s. 9d.

A further example from the *Dorset County Chronicle:*

The Mayor said he was a great animal lover, and he detested people who were cruel to animals. 'It is bad enough with children, but when it comes to dumb animals it is terrible,' he said.

And another from *The Lady:*

An entirely new development is the taking over the care of their own infants by young mothers of the aristocratic and cultivated sorts who have never before in history actually nursed their babies, though they have been expert and successful in the raising and training of animals.

This kind of attitude has a long history. William Penn wrote in the seventeenth century:

Men are generally more careful of the breed of their horses and dogs than of their children.

Well, animals are much easier than children. They are loyal and they're friendly and they don't answer back. People get very attached to their pets and find them a valuable source of company. From the *Manchester Evening Chronicle:*

> **Asked at Bedlington (Northumberland) Juvenile Court today to value his bantam hen stolen by boys, a 60-year-old witness replied: 'As a bird I value it at 5s, but as a friend I value it at 7s 6d.'**

An animal can give all elements of friendship except conversation. And even that is sometimes possible, according to this report from the *Evening News:*

> **A Portsmouth man believes he has found the way to talk to hedgehogs – although he does not know the meaning of what he says to them.**

It's not surprising that people are ready to believe that so-called dumb animals can speak, because many animals have other distinctly human characteristics. Cats, for instance. They are independent creatures whose attitude to their owners is always a bit difficult to assess. Montaigne on the subject:

> **When I play with my cat, who knows but that she regards me more as a plaything than I do her?**

Oliver Herford:

> **Cat: a pygmy lion, who loves mice, hates dogs, and patronizes human beings.**

But in spite of their patronizing, cats can be very entertaining, particularly when they're young. Henry David Thoreau:

> **A kitten is so flexible that she is almost double; the hind parts are equivalent to another kitten with which the forepart plays. She does not discover that her tail belongs to her until you tread upon it.**

Cats lead their own lives. They get around. Here's a useful tip from Barry Pain:

> **Buy visiting cards for the cat; she knows a lot more cats than we know people.**

The disadvantages of cats' independence is that they keep on getting lost, and their owners have to advertise in the newspapers in the hope of recovering them:

Lost, Tabby Cat, Male, answers to John. Reward (one black eye).

Missing, part-Persian cat, brown and orange. Finder rewarded, dead or alive.

Lost, ginger cat called Chips, answers to Fish.

If you don't like the idea of your pet wandering all over the place and patronizing you, perhaps you should get a dog instead. They are particularly popular as pets because of their proverbial devotion to their masters. It's so flattering. Holbrook Jackson:

Man is a dog's ideal of what God should be.

Aldous Huxley:

To his dog, every man is Napoleon; hence the constant popularity of dogs.

Here's another advantage of dog-owning, from Samuel Butler:

The great pleasure of a dog is that you may make a fool of yourself with him and not only will he not scold you, but he will make a fool of himself too.

Dogs feature quite as much as cats in the small ad columns of newspapers. Some examples:

Found. White Fox-terrier dog. Apply with name on collar, to 51, Park Road.

£25 reward to anyone finding red male chow dog or to anyone saying they killed this dog.

Collie dog, 1 year old, for sale, will work sheep or cattle, hunt out any distance and stop to whistle.

Some owners spend a lot of time washing and grooming their dogs, though not all authorities recommend this. Francis Galton:

Well-washed and well-combed domestic pets grow dull; they miss the stimulus of fleas.

Edward Noyes Westcott:

They say a reasonable amount o' fleas is good for a dog – keeps him broodin' over bein' a dog, mebbe.

But, fleas or not, dogs have their uses. They can be specially bred to look after sheep. A report from *The Scotsman:*

> **Let there be no misunderstanding. A mating of two champion sheep-dogs is more likely to produce a super Border Collie than the mating of two champion cattle or horses.**

Dogs are sometimes claimed to have almost supernatural powers in the judgment of character. They can be relied on to pick the goodies from the baddies. Josh Billings:

> **Money will buy a pretty good dog, but it won't buy the wag of his tail.**

Or, from a letter to *The Star:*

> **A dog usually possesses those fine qualities in which human beings are sometimes deficient. If your dog were suddenly to know you as you are, and not as he thinks you are, could you look him in the face?**

And from the *Sporting Weekly:*

> **The outstanding characteristic of the dog is its honesty. In love or hate, joy or sorrow, a dog is sincere. It will not bite your hand or wag its tail unless it likes you.**

There are those who reckon dogs and cats to be pretty boring pets and favour the more exotic of the world's species. For people of such tastes, I will close this chapter with a word of caution from Hilaire Belloc:

A python I should not advise,
It needs a doctor for its eyes,
And has the measles yearly.

However, if you feel inclined
To get one (to improve your mind,
And not from fashion merely),
Allow no music near its cage;
And when it flies into a rage
Chastise it, most severely.

I had an aunt in Yucatan
Who bought a python from a man
    And kept it for a pet.
She died, because she never knew
These simple little rules and few:—
The snake is living yet.

─HOLIDAYS─

'Ah,' said the businessman to his secretary, 'what a wonderful weekend we had in Brighton. Can you ever forget it?'

'What's it worth?' asked the girl.

There are always fortune-tellers at the seaside. Two of them met on the front at Frinton one sunny summer day. 'Lovely weather,' said the first fortune-teller.

'Yes,' said the second. 'It reminds me of the summer of 1986.'

Went to the seaside for a holiday last year. The landlady said to me, 'Our rates are five pounds a night, bed and breakfast — or four pounds if you make your own bed.'

'Oh, all right,' I said, 'I'll make the bed.'

And the landlady gave me a saw, a hammer and some nails.

Two little East End kids were paddling in the sea at Southend. 'Cor,' said one, 'look at your feet. They ain't half dirty.'

'Well, we didn't have no 'oliday last year.'

Went on holiday last week. What a week it was. Only rained twice — once for three days, once for four.

A poor little East End kid was taken away to the country for his first holiday and as he got out of the train at his destination he looked around in bewilderment. 'Blimey! What a lot of grass to keep off.'

Two seagulls were flying over the beach at a seaside resort one boiling hot August Bank Holiday afternoon. Every way they looked, there were so many people there wasn't a speck of sand to be seen.

'Ah,' said one to the other contemptuously, 'takes all the skill out of it, doesn't it?'

A Scot from Aberdeen was on holiday in London and every night he returned to his hotel full of the wonders of the city. So much so that another guest asked: 'Is this your first visit?'

'Aye, it is.'

'You seem to be having a great time.'

'Aye, I am that.'

'Good.'

'And what's more, it's not just a holiday. It's my honeymoon as well.'

'Oh. Then where's your wife?'

'Och. She's been here before.'

Holidays are almost always looked forward to. It's evidence of man's indomitable spirit or perpetual optimism or something, that no matter what disasters may befall people on one holiday, they still look forward to the next. It's the contrast that does it. The thought of two weeks that are different keeps the average worker going for the other fifty. As William Shakespeare says in *Henry IV, Part 1:*

If all the year were playing holidays,
To sport would be as tedious as to work;
But when they seldom come, they wish'd-for come.

The same thought is extended by George Bernard Shaw:

A perpetual holiday is a good working definition of hell.

But since not many of us can entertain the possibility of a perpetual holiday, we keep our illusions about the few weeks that are possible. And these illusions are fostered by the holiday travel industry, whose brochures seem to promise not only the beauties of nature, the gastronomic wonders of the world, sporting facilities unrivalled by Olympic stadia, but also the solution to all personal problems and the finding of perfect romance. Merely the cost of postage can fill your doormat with glossy portraits of paradise, and the day-dreams they stimulate are often more fun than the actual holiday.

Details of package tours always seem to be couched in superlatives, but the more sedate brochures of old-fashioned hotels are often sources of unintentional humour. Here are some examples:

Guests' dogs are charged 1s or 1s 6d per day according to size and social standing.

An additional attraction is fishing for guests, both game and coarse.

A stimulating start to the day is given by our enormous traditional breakfast served in the dining-room, or by a chambermaid in your bedroom.

Late dinners are a regular feature of our service.

Nowadays an increasing number of people go abroad for their holidays, and many are unprepared for the adjustment they have to make to the customs and manners of the country in which they arrive. It is fortunate that there are books available to instruct the traveller. Here is some handy advice from Baedeker's *Guide to the Mediterranean*, published in 1911:

> **Intercourse with Orientals.**
> The objects and pleasures of travel are so unintelligible to most Orientals that they are apt to regard the European traveller as a lunatic, or at all events a Croesus, and therefore to be exploited on every possible occasion. Hence their constant demands for 'bakshish' (a gift). To check this demoralizing cupidity the traveller should never give bakshish except for services rendered, unless occasionally to aged or crippled beggars.

Here's another useful tip from the 1902 version of Baedeker's *Egypt:*

> **The traveller [in Cairo and Alexandria] should keep his eye on the direction taken by the cab, as sometimes the cabman drives straight ahead in complete ignorance of the way and requires to be guided, e.g. by being touched with a stick on the right or left arm according to the turning.**

(That system of directions is not to be recommended with London cabbies.)

When thinking of holidays, there is, as I said, a growing tendency to ignore our own country in favour of somewhere more exotic. But we shouldn't forget the beauties on our doorstep. In recent years a more positive approach to attracting holiday-makers has developed. A report from the *Daily Mirror:*

A lead from the Corporation, a few pounds spent on gondolas, tables outside the waterside pubs, plenty of coloured lights, and Wigan, like Venice, could be taking in dollars from tourists.

The old deterrent to holidays in Britain is our unpredictable weather. But there may be a way round that.

Hotel-keepers and seaside caterers are watching the move made by Mr George Brenner, chairman of the Grand Pier Co., Weston-Super-Mare, who is investigating the possibility of legal action to restrain the BBC from broadcasting 'discouraging' weather forecasts.

Another regular feature of seaside holidays in Britain is the seaside postcard, complete with enormous busty ladies, little weedy

'THE TIDE'S OUT, SO HOW CAN YOU HEAR THE SEA SLAPPING AGAINST THE ROCKS?'

men wearing braces and knotted handkerchiefs on their heads, and dubious goings-on in bathing-huts.

In a similar vein is that other popular form of humour — the landlady joke. There are millions of them, but all with the same central figure – the dragon of a landlady who runs her guest-house like a prison-camp with hundreds of impossible rules. Here are a few specimen jokes:

> **A man was being shown round the guest-house by the landlady.**
>
> **'This is your room. Any complaints?'**
>
> **'Well, the window's a bit small. Wouldn't be much use in an emergency.'**
>
> **'There won't be an emergency,' said the landlady. 'My terms are cash in advance.'**

'Excuse me,' said the guest, 'but this steak is so tough I can't even cut it. Take it away and bring me another.'

'I can't take it away,' said the landlady. 'You've bent it.'

A holidaymaker was complaining to his landlady about his room. 'Look. This wall's so thin you can almost see through it.'

'That's not a wall,' she replied, 'it's the window.'

A man arrived at his holiday guest-house and met the landlady.

'Can you sing?' she snapped.

'No,' he replied.

'Well, you'd better learn quickly. There's no lock on the loo.'

And a last thought on rules and regulations in guest-houses from a member of the Morecambe Hotels and Caterers Association, quoted in the *Morecambe Guardian:*

> **I have found that if you don't lock the bathroom some people are taking baths every day.**

Shocking. With such delights at home it's amazing that people want to travel overseas. Certainly a lot of eminent men would tend to discourage them. Thomas Nashe, for instance, writing in the sixteenth century:

> **Countriman, tell me, what is the occasion of thy straying so farre out of England, to visit this strange nation? If it bee languages, thou maist lerne them at home; nought but lasciviousnesse is to bee learnt here.**

G. K. Chesterton:

> **It is a pity that people travel in foreign countries; it narrows their minds so much.**

TERRORS OF THE SCOTTISH LANGUAGE.

Housemaid in Glasgow Hotel. 'Ye canna gang to the bathroom the noo.'
Sassenach. 'Why not?' *Housemaid.* 'There's a body in the bath.'

George V:

> **I hate abroad.**

And a typically crushing line from Dr Johnson:

> **A blade of grass is always a blade of grass, whether in one country or another.**

Some Britishers attempt to dilute the foreign-ness of being abroad. Here's a letter published in the *Leicester Mercury:*

> **We went to France for our holidays and took six large sliced loaves of bread with us. We still had one left after 13 days. It was still good to eat. This is a tribute to a Leicester bakery.**

But food is not the only problem on foreign holidays. An anecdote from Frances Trollope, the mother of Anthony Trollope:

> **I remember being much amused last year, when landing at Calais, at the answer made by an old traveller to a novice who was making his first voyage. 'What a dreadful smell!' said the uninitiated stranger, enveloping his nose in his pocket handkerchief.**
>
> **'It is the smell of the continent, sir,' replied the man of experience. And so it was.**

And so it still is.

If you travel abroad you have to decide what form of transport to take. Is it worth going by car and filling in all of the forms and things that that entails? And vying with all those mad foreign drivers? An extract from the *Irish Press:*

> **As an experiment in night traffic control, the white-cloaked traffic policeman at the Place de l'Alma in**

Paris is now being floodlit to ensure that night drivers will not miss him in the dark.

When one is abroad it is essential to behave well, but of course never to forget that one is British. A word of advice from *Manners for Women*, written by Mrs C.E. Humphrey in 1897:

It ought to be part of our patriotic feeling to endeavour to convey as agreeable an idea as possible of ourselves to those countries which we honour with our distinguished presence in our little trips.

Yes, dignity is important. One must never forget G.K. Chesterton's distinction between a traveller and a tripper:

The traveller sees what he sees; the tripper sees what he has come to see.

And on that note I'll close this chapter on Holidays – and indeed this book of *Going Into* . . . I hope you've enjoyed it.